THE
SCANDAL
OF
LENT

Themes for Lenten Preaching
in the Gospel of John

Robert Kysar

AUGSBURG Publishing House • Minneapolis

THE SCANDAL OF LENT

MANUFACTURED IN THE UNITED STATES OF AMERICA

CONTENTS

Introduction: The Scandal of Lent 5

Ash Wednesday: The Scandal of Rebirth (John 3:1-12) ... 8

First Week: The Scandal of Witness (John 1:43-51) 19

Second Week: The Scandal of Belief (John 2:12-22) 31

Third Week: The Scandal of Sensuality (John 6:53-58) 41

Fourth Week: The Scandal of Heaven on Earth
(John 5:21-27) 53

Fifth Week: The Scandal of Self-Hatred (John 12:25) 66

Maundy Thursday: The Scandal of Servanthood
(John 13:1-17) 76

Good Friday: The Scandal of Crucifixion (John 3:13-15) ... 87

Easter: The Scandal of Doubt (John 20:24-29) 97

Introduction:
The Scandal of Lent

The wedding vows taken at the altar are tenuous at best unless the couple has each seen one another at their worst. Until each has seen the other's faults and weaknesses, the pledge "to love and to cherish" is a hollow one. But when they truly know one another, "warts and all," the expressions of love can have authenticity. Maybe something like this is what Paul knew when he so poignantly wrote, "We preach Christ crucified, a stumbling block to Jews and folly to Gentiles" (1 Cor. 1:23). Paul knew that there was an offensive side to Christian faith and that there was no way faith could be genuine until that offense was squarely faced. Christian faith is trust over against that which would make it seem unbelievable. A crucified messiah presented a tremendous hurdle for the Jew of the first century, and the whole idea of such was sheer nonsense to the Greek persons of the day, endowed as they were with their great heritage of learning and reasonableness. So Paul chose his words with care—a "stumbling block" and "folly." Actually, the Greek word Paul used, "stumbling block," could more simply be rendered, "scandal." Paul understood the scandalous dimension of the Christian faith.

Unfortunately for many of us, however, that scandal has been minimized. Accustomed as we are to the tenets of Christian belief, nurtured in the atmosphere of the community of faith since our early years, and knowing the truth of the gospel message, many of us have become numbed to that dimension of which Paul speaks in the first chapter of 1 Corinthians. We are so close to our faith, and it is so intimately tied up with our lives, that we fail to see what a scandal it presents to the world. It is like the married couple who after years of living together and sharing their lives are almost unconscious of each other's faults. Love and intimacy have overcome the awareness of any shortcomings. And should a glaring fault in one surface in an obvious way, it only becomes the occasion for the other to affirm love all the more strongly. But in a sense it is always healthy for a married couple to be reminded of one another's faults, for it enables them to declare their love in spite of the faults—"for better, for worse." In much the same way, it is well for Christians to acknowledge again and again the scandal of God's act in Christ. Not that it is a fault in God's activity, but because— like the fault in a spouse—it occasions the declaration of faith in a *pure* way.

The presupposition of this book is that unless one is scandalized by the gospel message, she or he can never embrace it with authentic faith. So long as we remain blind to the truly ridiculous character of the Word of God made flesh and of a suffering and dying messiah, we have not completed that process which is the road from unbelief to faith. Some of us have never been brought face to face with that offiense; others of us confronted it once and chose to believe but through the years have allowed the awareness of that offense to dim. My contention is that when that awareness dims, so does the authenticity of our faith.

Søren Kierkegaard said it well for his age. He suggested that in a culture that is predominantly Christian we tend to make pablum of Christianity. We reduce it to the most easily digested form possible. For the purity of our faith, we must be newly impressed by the intellectual and existential offense of the gospel.

This book is designed to draw us back to the reality of that offense. It is intended to sketch the points at which Jesus most radically challenges our refined sensibilities but asks us nonetheless to believe. The first goal of the book is, then, to nurture faith. It attempts to evoke from the reader a response to Christ— either belief or disbelief.

The second goal of this book is to lead our thinking through the Lenten period by capturing some of the Lenten resources of the gospel of John. Much of the church's traditional Lenten observances are fashioned around the pattern of the last weeks in the life of Jesus as portrayed by the gospels of Matthew, Mark, and Luke. The result is that the gospel of John (except for selected passages) is pushed back for later reading and contemplation. This customary practice is a loss, I believe, for the gospel of John is rich with challengingly new and different expressions of Lenten themes. The gospel we will be studying focuses our attention upon some new shades of meaning in the fresco of Jesus' ministry, and I hope to draw the brilliance of those colors to your attention.

It was Paul who articulated explicitly the idea that there is a scandalous dimension to the Christian gospel. But his colleague in our New Testament, John, without ever using the word, portrays more vividly the specifics of that scandal. It is the scandal of Christian faith in general, but especially the scandal of Lent; for in the Lenten season the heart of the gospel emerges most forcefully to confront us and to ask us a question Jesus posed to his disciples. At the time, many were falling away, unable to respond in faith to the bold claims Jesus was making of himself. And so the disciples were asked, "Will you also go away?" It is my prayer that this book will enable some to answer with Peter: "Lord, to whom shall we go? You have the words of eternal life; and we have believed, and have come to know, that you are the Holy One of God" (John 6:67-69).

Ash Wednesday:
The Scandal of Rebirth

John 3:1-12

We hear much today about being "born again." The label, "born-again Christian," has been employed by some to distinguish themselves as some sort of special type of Christian. While not all who would gladly use this title for themselves are guilty of this, many would seem to say that they hold some greater claim to Christian authenticity than do others. William James years ago, however, distinguished between what he called, "once-born" and "twice-born" Christian believers. The point of his distinction was to acknowledge that some Christians grow gradually into mature belief while others experience a rather abrupt "conversion experience."

With all the publicity given to the "born-again Christians," it is necessary to remind ourselves that their entrance to the world of faith is but one of the routes and holds no special claim to authenticity. As a matter of fact, perhaps the so-called, "once-born" Christians ought to speak of their many experiences as rebirths. Many of those of us nurtured over the years in the Christian faith have been reborn not once but numerous times in our process of growth.

THE BIBLICAL CONCEPT OF REPENTANCE

The attention given to the "born-again" Christian does, however, draw our consideration to the fact that the Christian claims his or her life has been altered as a result of the grace of God. It brings to our consciousness the necessity of a turning about of the individual's life (whether that be a slow and gradual process or an abrupt one). And it is that process of being turned around that is the subject of this meditation for Ash Wednesday.

The passage in the gospel of John which speaks so vividly and provocatively of that process is the conversation between Jesus and Nicodemus found in Chapter 3. To focus our attention on this passage on Ash Wednesday may seem at first glance unusual. We are accustomed to hear of *repentance* spoken of as the essence of this solemn festival with which we begin the Lenten season. The gospel of John is, however, strangely silent when it comes to the matter of repentance. Shocking though it is, we find that John did not use the word, *repent* or *repentance,* even once in his entire gospel! If the theme of repentance is the essential meaning of Ash Wednesday, why focus our thoughts upon a passage from the gospel of John for this occasion?

The answer is simple: John goes to the heart of the meaning of repentance without ever using the word. He captures the sense of repentance in other words—words which are perhaps even more powerful than the time-worn phrases about repentance. The biblical concept of repentance involves a change of one's life center.

In the Old Testament the Hebrew word which is most often translated repentance is properly understood as "facing in another direction." It suggests that the people are moving in their lives in one direction and are asked to do an about-face and move in the opposite direction. That Old Testament theme is captured in the New Testament with a Greek word which literally means, "to change one's mind." But the concept of *mind* in Greek thought was not as limited as ours. The mind was for them the entire inner disposition of a person. We would say, perhaps, the *personality*. Consequently, *repentance* in the New Testament means a change of the innermost person, or the change of the basis of one's life.

The biblical concept of repentance might be represented in this sort of an analogy: modern methods of treating alcoholism have focused on the total person. Alcoholism cannot be successfully treated as a sort of unfortunate habit into which one has fallen. It is a disease, arising from the emotional makeup of the individual. Therapists today speak of "addictive personalities," meaning that there are individuals whose personalities make them particularly susceptible to dependence on a conscious-altering substance of some sort. They are people who for some reason have learned early in their lives to cope with difficult situations by escaping confrontation in one way or another. Consequently, alcoholism is viewed as a symptom of an underlying personality problem.

Successful treatment, then, involves not simply the process of helping people to free themselves from their destructive habit. It necessitates a basic kind of personality orientation. It must teach people to deal with difficulties rather than trying to escape from them. Thus, successful alcoholism treatment involves a radical change of the inner person. It involves, we would even say, *repentance* in the biblical sense; for it requires individuals to undergo a foundational change in their way of viewing life. It is this kind of reordering of one's life that the Bible has in mind when it speaks of repentance.

In the popular reduction of repentance to a sense of feeling sorry for wrongs we have done, we have lost a good deal of the biblical concept of repentance. To be sure, the turning around or the radical change of one's inner life basis would involve an element of regret and even sorrow. But the focus of the word is toward the positive change called for in repentance, not the feeling of sadness for the past. It is a forward-looking word. A word that points us toward what we are to *be,* not toward what we have *done* in the past.

REBIRTH IN JOHN

The writer of the Fourth Gospel chooses to speak of this drastic turnabout with other words than repentance. But speak of it he does with exciting word pictures which grip the imagination and stir the emotions. John is then an appropriate subject for our Ash Wednesday reflection, if only because he forces us to rethink our conception of repentance along lines which are more faithfully biblical.

John speaks of this dramatic change occasioned by the act of God in Christ in the context of his report of the conversation between Nicodemus and Jesus. A fascinating character, this Nicodemus. We hear of him only in the gospel of John and then on only three occasions: 3:1-12; 7:50-52; 19:39.

Who was this Nicodemus? It appears that, like Joseph of Arimathea, he was a secret believer and follower of Jesus, who, because of his fear of others, was cautious about making his belief a public matter. He may have been a person who was so involved in the religious establishment of the day that he feared the scandal of becoming identified with a popular religious movement condemned by the establishment. In portraying Nicodemus John may have had in mind those members of the Jewish synagogue in his own community who secretly had affinities with the Christian movement but were not bold enough to make their opinions known. To do so, of course, would have meant exclusion from the synagogue. So Nicodemus may be for John the representative of those who could not bring themselves to sacrifice their ties with their heritage in order to embrace the Christian faith. He would be not unlike those persons today who find their tendency toward Christian belief an embarrassment and a threat to their social position. On the other hand, let's be fair to Nicodemus. In the end he came forward to assist in the burial of Jesus. Does that suggest that he finally found the courage to identify himself with this scandalous person, Jesus of Nazareth? Or are we to assume that he aided in the burial in the same manner he had come to Jesus originally—under the cover of darkness?

His initial conversation with Jesus about which John tells us in Chapter 3 indicates that he was a person of prominence ("a ruler of the Jews") who came to Jesus "by night." And it is obvious that he holds Jesus in high respect: "Rabbi, we know that you are a teacher come from God." Certainly this is no confession of faith in Jesus, but it is an expression of profound respect. According to John, Jesus quickly moves the discussion to a weighty matter: "Truly, truly, I say to you, unless one is born anew, he cannot see the kingdom of God" (v. 3).

But Nicodemus is totally dumbfounded by those words of Jesus and entirely misunderstands him. In innocent misunderstanding he asks how an elderly person can be expected to reenter his mother's womb to be born again. Jesus must go on to say that the birth of which he speaks is a birth of the Spirit (and of water) and proceeds to speak of how the Spirit gives a rebirth. Still, Nicodemus does not understand (v. 9). Jesus rebukes him a bit: "Are you a teacher of Israel, and yet you do not understand this?"

This wise religious leader, respected by the devout of his day, is utterly at a loss to understand what it is Jesus is saying. As we shall point out in a later chapter, John is fond of having the listeners of Jesus fail to grasp the meaning of his words. Their misunderstanding is an occasion for John to have Jesus expand his original remarks and suggests the failure of the world to comprehend the message of God embodied in the person of Jesus. But with Nicodemus the technique of misunderstanding is especially powerful, for it suggests how this theme of radical reorientation of life catches us off guard. Those most likely to understand are still at a loss to grasp what it is Jesus is saying. But it may be that John wants us to know too that Nicodemus *did not really want* to hear and understand what Jesus was saying.

The scandal of Jesus' insistence that we must be born again is that it means we must put aside our claims to self-accomplishment and status. This is not a blatantly sinful man to whom

Jesus is speaking. Nicodemus is no lost soul, squandering his life in the pleasures of the world. He is no impious fool who has refused to acknowledge God's sovereignty in this world. On the contrary, he is a cultured, devout, learned, and respected member of his community. By the standards of his day, he had "arrived." He had accomplished what few could hope for in their time. He had devoted himself (we may assume) to the teachings of the Old Testament Law and as a Pharisee observed them meticulously. Yet it is to him that Jesus says, "Unless one is born anew, he cannot see the kingdom of God." There is a radical turnabout demanded even of one who has devoted himself so intensely to God as has Nicodemus. Nicodemus perhaps could not understand Jesus' words because he could not think of himself as one who needed to be changed in any drastic sense.

REBIRTH IS NOT AN ACCOMPLISHMENT

The first scandal of the idea of rebirth is in the claim that our accomplishments are not enough. Nicodemus perhaps thought that he was doing everything that was necessary. But the words of Jesus insist that *what he has done is not the point.* Nicodemus was in one world, and Jesus in another. Nicodemus was in the world of accomplishment, and Jesus was asking him to leave that world and enter the realm of grace.

The idea of a rebirth is no less scandalous to our ears today, for many of us live in that world of accomplishment. In spite of the gospel message that we have heard many times over, many of us still contend secretly that it is what we *do* which finally allows us to see the kingdom of God. It is not the case, therefore, that Nicodemus has trouble grasping Jesus' words because he is a Jew or even a Pharisee. He is troubled and confused by the words he hears because as a human being he is caught up in the syndrome so common to us all—the syndrome of accomplishment.

We live in the world of accomplishment. We are trained from our earliest years that what we gain in life we gain through our own hard work. Like a computer we are programmed to think that way from the earliest of years, until finally we unconsciously embrace a view of ourselves which necessitates that we think in terms of what we have accomplished. If we cannot point to those accomplishments with pride, we may feel that we are somehow inadequate or deficient. Our society rewards those who accomplish and looks with disfavor upon those who do not. Woven into the fabric of our personalities are the threads of the work ethic. Why are there so many "workaholics" among us? Why are there so many plagued with persistent tension and ulcers? Why are the mental wards filled with those of us who have suffered what we continue euphemistically to call, "nervous breakdowns," and other wards occupied with persons recovering from exhaustion? Is it not, in part at least, because we insist upon evaluating ourselves by the norm of what we have accomplished and forever drive ourselves to accomplish still more and more?

It is scandalous from the point of view of our society that Jesus should say to an "accomplished person" like Nicodemus, "Unless one is born anew, he cannot see the kingdom of God." If it were to a lazy, unmotivated person that Jesus said these words, we would be able to understand. But by the standards of our society Nicodemus was one who was on the right track; he did not need to be turned around. The offense of Jesus' words is that they strike at the very foundation of our culture. The scandal of the rebirth about which Jesus speaks is that it requires us to think differently about what is most important in life. And that is just like this Jesus, for he was prone to upset the standard norm (see, for instance, Mark 9:35; 10:31; Matt. 5:5; and Luke 6:20). He pulls the rug out from under our cultural norms; he chips away with his radical teachings at the very foundations of our society. The scandal of rebirth is that we are asked to surrender our commitment to an accomplishment-oriented life.

REBIRTH IS A GIFT

But the scandal of these words goes further. The turnabout that Jesus demands involves not only our letting go of our compulsive drive to succeed. It involves allowing something to be done for us. Jesus insists that the rebirth is a birth from above. The Greek word can be translated both, "anew" (as it is in the text of the RSV) or "from above" (as it is in the footnote of the RSV). The second birth is a birth from another realm, from the divine realm. We are to receive this new orientation of our lives from the work of God, and not from our own efforts. Rudolf Schnackenburg, a prominent Roman Catholic New Testament scholar, comments on this passage with these words: "Prior to all human effort to attain to the kingdom of God, God himself must create the basis of a new being in man, which will also make a new way of life possible" (*The Gospel According to St. John,* Vol. I, p. 368). Jesus furthers this point when he insists that the birth he is talking about is a birth of the Spirit.

The concept of the Spirit of God in the gospel of John is a rich and profound one. But for now he gives us only some fundamentals of the concept of the Spirit. In a little analogy of wind and spirit he stresses the freedom of the Spirit: "the wind [or spirit] blows where it wills, and you hear the sound of it, but you do not know whence it comes or whither it goes." Like the wind, the Spirit of God is beyond our control. We are unable to command the wind to blow when and in the direction we desire. Even with our advanced technology, the wind remains a free agent, beyond our control. Neither is the Spirit of God within our control. All that we might do cannot make the Spirit subject to our command. This means, we should add, that even our piety does not subject the Spirit to our will. Our prayers and our services of worship do not function as a control panel for the directing of the Spirit. John has Jesus emphasizing the absolute freedom of the Spirit of God.

But the metaphor concerning the wind and the Spirit of God also suggests that there is always a dimension of mystery about the Spirit. "You hear the sound of it [the wind], but you do not know whence it comes or whither it goes." Where does the wind come from? Where does it go? You do not see the wind, yet you see its effects as it blows the trees, unfurls the flag, and tugs at our bodies. The wind is mysterious in its comings and goings and in its unseen power. So it is with the Spirit of God, John suggests. The Spirit remains a mystery, even for the Christian. God's Spirit is his unseen presence, which nonetheless manifests itself in power. It comes mysteriously and goes mysteriously.

If you have ever had the experience of sailing, you know what John is saying. While sailing, you remain entirely at the mercy of the wind. You may capture the wind in your sails for a time, but you know that it may disappear suddenly, leaving you stranded in the middle of the lake. You may capture the wind in your sails for a time and use it to move you in the direction you want to go, but you know that it may shift directions without warning, leaving you unable to proceed in the direction you desire to go. Sailing makes one acutely aware of the freedom of the wind and its mysterious character. You cannot sail long before developing a profound respect for the wind and its power. Like the wind, the Spirit of God is free and mysterious.

It is the Spirit of God, John says, that gives the rebirth about which Jesus speaks to Nicodemus. From another realm beyond this world the Spirit enters our lives and turns us around. The inescapable conclusion of what Jesus says about the birth from above is that it is a *gift,* given out of God's freedom and given mysteriously. And that is just the scandal of the rebirth about which Jesus speaks. It is not something *we do. It is something that is done for us by the Spirit of God.* The scandalous idea of the new birth is that we cannot accomplish it the way we work hard and gain a promotion in our job or earn a degree or merit an award or win a contest. It is a gift given without consideration of prior accomplishments or attainments. That is what made Jesus' words so hard for Nicodemus to grasp, and that is what makes these words difficult for us to hear. Not even by our act of repentance do we necessarily gain this radical turn-about that John has in mind. Not by all our prayers, not by all our deeds of love, not by our polished liturgies, not by our learned theologies. The radical repentance which John has in mind here as he has Jesus describe the rebirth is a transformation for which we are utterly dependent on the Spirit of God.

We don't like being dependent. We don't even like receiving gifts. Most of us when we receive a gift feel uncomfortable about it until we have had the opportunity to give our benefactor something in return. That is so because we are an accomplishment- and work-oriented people. We want to earn everything we have. We feel uncomfortable with an unearned gift precisely because that makes us feel dependent and indebted to the other person. The precise offense of the Johannine idea of rebirth is that it is an unearned gift which can never be repaid.

Such an idea is emotionally disturbing, and so we have done strange things to this concept of rebirth. Most obviously we have turned it into something that we humans do by our decision of faith. We have tried to make it a matter dependent upon the decision of our wills. It is a matter of what we may accomplish by *our* decision and by *our* faith. But that understanding of the rebirth turns a deaf ear to the really offensive nature of these words of Jesus. The real offense is that we can do little or nothing to accomplish this rebirth. It is the work of the Spirit of God.

Of course, the rebirth of which Jesus speaks is a gift, and we do have the power to say no to a gift. If a friend offers us a gift, it is in our power to say, "No, thank you anyway!" We can say *no* to the Spirit of God; that is a power we have. But the power to earn the gift, to solicit it, to oblige the Spirit of God to bestow it—that is a power we do not have.

The reason this rebirth must be a gift of God and not the work of us humans is simple: the rebirth is actually a re-creation. It is not a mere realignment of the human person, not a tampering with the human disposition which can be done with human efforts, and not a remodeling of the old person with a new coat of paint and a fresh facade. No, this rebirth is a new creation.

And only God creates new persons. "Therefore, if any one is in Christ, he is a new creation; the old has passed away, behold, the new has come" (2 Cor. 5:17). As God once created the human with the power of his word, "Let us make man in our image. . ." (Gen. 1:26), now he creates the new human through a rebirth by the power of his Spirit.

If this indeed be the Johannine concept of repentance, how drastically different it is from ours. It is a change of the inner nature that we cannot effect of our own efforts, but one for which we can only yearn and wait patiently. In a society that says, "Go, make something of yourself," the Johannine concept of rebirth comes as a shock. For it says, "Let God make something of you." Like Nicodemus, we will not want to hear these words. We will try, instead, to hear Jesus saying, "Repent, believe, and you are born again." But John's offensive words will not budge! There they are: hard rocks for us to knock our independent, accomplishment-oriented heads against.

"Unless one is born anew, he cannot see the kingdom of God. . . . Unless one is born of water and the Spirit, he cannot enter the kingdom of God." What shall we do with these words? Let's misunderstand them, as Nicodemus did. That will be more comfortable for us. Better, let's accept the fact that our rebirth is the work of the Spirit of God and that we can only open our lives to receive the gift of that drastic reorientation when the Spirit is ready to bestow it.

First Week:
The Scandal of Witness

John 1:43-51

THE SCANDAL OF WITNESS

Selling has become an established profession in our society, and some would even say that selling is an art. There are certainly skills involved. Those of us who are not salespersons by vocation and have been in a position of having to try to sell someone something know how valuable those special skills are. From the other end of the process, buying a used car from a private party is often almost humorous. The person selling the car may attempt to mimic the sales techniques of the professional and make a fool of himself or herself; or, they may be so vastly different from the professional as to make us laugh. And indeed, selling may even be an art. To know the precise time to "push" the customer or when to ease off, to "psyche out" the customer and make the sales approach that will most effectively reach her or him—those are matters which may almost qualify good selling as an art.

It is often the case that the church and the pastor are spoken of in terms of selling a product. More than once someone has said to me, "You pastors are really salespersons, aren't you? You're trying to sell religion." And some of the techniques advocated for the witness of the church are clearly and openly modeled after those which have been developed in the business world.

How can the church be effective in this modern age unless it begins to use some of the polished, proven, and appealing approaches developed in successful sales agencies?

Common sense tells us that this is the case. And yet when we look at the New Testament and examine the means of witnessing employed there by the earliest of Christians, we blush in embarrassment. The most colossal failure of the apostle Paul in his efforts to witness to the gospel before the Gentiles may have been when it appears he came closest to using the techniques of modern selling (Acts 17:22-33). Faced with an audience of Athenians, Paul tried to fit his message to the interests and ways of thinking of these intellectually sophisticated persons. But by the time Paul is forced to get around to the content of the gospel itself, he alienates his audience with the reference to the resurrection of Christ (v. 31). At this some of his listeners mock him, and it appears that Paul's ministry in Athens is for all effect ended. The truth of the matter is that the early Christians were enthusiastic and vigorous in their witness, but, alas, they were not very good salespersons by our standards.

JOHN'S VIEW OF CHRISTIAN WITNESS

The story of Philip and his efforts to bring Nathanael to Jesus is a provocative commentary on Christian witness. Our passage for this first week of Lent is found in the context of what has often been called the Johannine version of the calling of the disciples. It begins with the witness of John the Baptist to Jesus (1:19-34), and the effect of the Baptizer's witness is that two of his own disciples follow Jesus (vv. 35-39). They in turn are successful in getting others to join the followers of Jesus (vv. 40-42). Then in verse 43 Jesus invites Philip into the circle of disciples, and Philip in turn brings Nathanael to Jesus. The whole scene climaxes in Nathanael's experience with Jesus, his confession of faith, and Jesus' enticing words concerning what is in store for the disciples (vv. 47-51).

Our passage is probably the evangelist's retelling of a tale which might have originally been a little sermon. If you read 1:19-51 carefully, you see a number of interesting things. The first is the whole series of titles which are used of Jesus spread throughout the passage and culminating in Nathanael's confession in verse 49 and Jesus' (apparent) correction of that confession with the title, "Son of man."

But, second, you will notice in reading these verses the recurrence of the words, "Come and see," and "follow." Originally the passage may have been a sermon in which the preacher described the experience of these disciples in being brought into the circle of followers of Jesus. The preacher probably hoped to lead his listeners into a similar kind of experience. However, one is struck by the relative passivity of Jesus. He does nothing to attract attention. He speaks briefly on only a couple of occasions. Everything in this account of the calling of the disciples depends on the power of witness: the witness of the Baptizer and then of those others who have encountered Jesus. The result is that at the hand of the evangelist this story has been transformed into a brief introduction to the role of Christian witness and the confessions about the identity of Christ which arise because of witness. John, indeed, may have wanted this little portion of his gospel to serve as an instructional manual for Christian witness. Not very impressive when compared to the elaborate aids with which the church trains lay persons for witness today, with the flip-charts and all the rest. But it is just that stark contrast with the techniques of the contemporary church and its evangelistic efforts that makes John's story before us most intriguing.

In a very carefully calculated way, I believe, John is presenting us here with the scandalous task of Christian witness. In particular, I think, the scandal of witness for John in this passage is really twofold.

THE SCANDAL OF HUMBLE ORIGINS

The first dimension of the scandal of witness in John 1:43-51 is the fact that we must witness to one of such extremely humble origins. John's account of the calling of the disciples and the effectiveness of witness sails along beautifully until the episode in which Philip invites Nathanael to join the circle of followers (vv. 43ff). Nathanael resists the invitation. To the suggestion that Jesus of Nazareth is the one "of whom Moses in the law and also the prophets wrote," Nathanael responds curtly, "Can anything good come out of Nazareth?" That remark has engendered a great deal of scholarly discussion. Does Nathanael here recite a proverb which expressed the general disdain in which Nazareth was held by the people of Galilee? If Nathanael is from Cana as 21:2 suggests, is his remark a reflection on a rivalry between the two neighboring villages of Cana and Nazareth?

Let's assume that Nathanael is a bit more learned and means by his comment that it is not likely the promised Prophet-Messiah of the Old Testament should originate in the tiny village of Nazareth. Nazareth is nowhere mentioned as a place of religious importance in the Old Testament and apparently played no role in the speculation about whence the Messiah would come. As a matter of fact, Galilee in general was not thought to be a possible root for the long-expected Prophet-Messiah (7:52). We could further speculate that Nathanael knew the tradition that the origin of the Messiah would be obscure until the last moment. The Messiah would, according to some Jewish speculation, live among the people for a time unrecognized and unknown, until he would at last reveal himself to Israel.

All of this is very interesting, but the point is far more simple and clear. Nathanael has difficulty with the thought that the Messiah would originate from such humble surroundings as the village of Nazareth. Surely the long-awaited warrior, king, and savior would not come from the puny environment of such a locale. It is the same objection we hear voiced in 6:42 of John.

Jesus claims to be the bread from heaven and his listeners wonder in amazement: "He is no more from heaven than you or I. We even know his parents. He is the son of Joseph." John 6:42 expresses the inability of the crowd to distinguish the worldly (physical) origin of Jesus and his heavenly (spiritual) origin. Nathanael's objection is similar: the Messiah is not to arise from such demeaning surroundings.

The same mentality is present in our own age but in a different way. We marvel and even become sentimental over the thought that a great leader of our nation should arise from humble surroundings. That Lincoln should be born in a log cabin in Kentucky and go on to become president of the nation captures our imaginations because of its unlikelihood. Jimmy Carter made much of his simple origins as a southern peanut farmer in his rise to political prominence. We do not expect greatness to originate from humble surroundings, and when it does, it stirs our admiration and respect.

But with Nathanael we are dealing with a more stubborn resistance. His imagination is not captured by this claim made by Philip. Nathanael does not feel a swelling of admiration and respect for one who might come from Nazareth to be recognized as the Prophet-Messiah. On the contrary, he is overwhelmed by disbelief. God would not allow his special redemptive agent to make his worldly appearance in the measly setting of a village like Nazareth. That would be like discovering a jewel in the midst of a vein of coal or a gold watch in a garbage can! Such humble origins are inconceivable, knowing the destiny of the Messiah.

Philip is confronted with the task of overcoming the scandal of the humble origins of this one whom he believes to be the fulfillment of the Jewish expectations of the Prophet-Messiah. How to convince the disbelieving Nathanael that *in spite* of Jesus' origins he is nonetheless the One for whom they had waited? Especially difficult is the task, since common sense (along with scholarly speculation) dictated that the Messiah would have an origin which would befit his office.

But Nathanael is not stumbling over a mere technicality! He is restrained from believing the words of Philip by a serious and fundamental offense in God's act in Christ. As Rudolf Bultmann has so well said, "It seems incredible to Nathanael that obscure Nazareth could be the home of the promised one. But—as the reader must learn—God's action is surprising and incredible; and the offense of the Messiah's coming from Nazareth belongs, as the Evangelist understands it, to the offense of the incarnation of the Logos" (*The Gospel of John,* pp. 103-104). The difficulty of belief experienced by Nathanael is part and parcel of the whole package of God's revelation in Jesus of Nazareth. For Nathanael it was Nazareth that offended him; for us it is the whole idea of God's acting through one whose historical setting was so unexpected. It is not only surprising; it is unbelievable!

The scandal of the Christian witness is that it points to a figure who by historical standards is microscopic. We witness to one who lived and worked not at the center of historical events, but far out on the fringe. Would that Jesus were a figure of prominence in one of the historical powers of civilization! Would he had been born in Rome and participated in the world-changing events of history in that mighty empire, but not in puny Israel! The burden of the Christian witness is to convince the doubtful that God could act in a way that transformed history while in effect ignoring the powers of historical change themselves!

How shall we overcome this offensive burden? Shall we argue that history is full of surprises of which the birth of Jesus in tiny Judah is but one? For instance, shall we argue that it is comparable to the fact that World War I was precipitated by the assassination of the archduke of Austria-Hungary by an obscure Serbian nationalist in 1914? Or shall we claim that it was an event that disclosed the real, although heretofore hidden power of history in much the same way that the oil embargo of the Arabic nations in 1973 suddenly made the western world conscious of the significance of those small nations?

To be sure, history is dotted with such surprises. But such an argument seems frail in comparison with the offense presented to us by the appearance of the Christ in Galilee. Shall we instead argue that this appearance is anticipated in the Old Testament by means of its "prophecies"? Matthew and Luke seem intent on this course in their recounting of the birth of Jesus. For example, each in his own unique way argues that Jesus was actually born in Bethlehem, although raised in Nazareth—this in order to tie Jesus with the popular understanding of the role of Bethlehem in Old Testament prophecies (see Luke 2:1-7 and Matt. 2:1-6). Indeed, we cannot demean this approach to understanding the origins of Jesus, for it seems to have been one of the primary weapons employed by the early church in its evangelistic efforts. And yet it is instructive that neither Paul nor John appeals to such arguments to bypass the implicit offense of Jesus' origins.

John seems intent on just the opposite. He seems not to want to weaken or diminish the incredibility of the claim that the Messiah originated in Nazareth. John's approach is not to relegate it to one of the surprises of history or to authenticate Jesus' origins on Old Testament grounds. Rather, he would have us face it squarely as one of the unbelievable surprises of God's total act in Christ. To follow John's path is to say that this bold fact is not to be skirted but to be encountered head-on. The Christian witness has two options: one is to try to make the presentation of the Christian faith appear as reasonable as possible and to minimize the offensive character of the Christian proclamation. That option is a noble one, pursued by many in the history of the Christian church. The other option is to make the presentation of the Christian faith in spite of its inherent scandal to the modern mind. This option pursues with confidence the conviction that belief alone overcomes that which appears unreasonable and unbelievable about the proclamation.

The choice is like that of the salesperson, if I may invoke a crude analogy: the nature of the product may be presented accurately and without defense in the belief (to quote the phrase so often used) that the product "sells itself." Or, an elaborate defense of the product can be constructed—a defense that makes all of the unattractiveness of the product pale in the presence of its worth. Such an analogy is fraught with difficulties, but the point is that John felt that Christian witness must allow the Christ figure "to sell himself." To do otherwise is to miss the core of the meaning of what God has done in this figure.

The scandal of Christian witness is that we must continue to point to a figure with the meagerest of origins and to claim that figure is the supreme act of God for the salvation of humankind. We can do no other! We cannot compromise the offensiveness of that witness, because the appeal of faith takes root in that very offensiveness. The Christian witness cannot minimize the scandal of Christ's origins in the name of making the appeal more reasonable and believable, because the Christian gospel does not present itself on the basis of its reasonableness and credibility for the human mind. Its ground for appeal is one simple fact: it is the truth of God.

THE SCANDAL OF
THE INVITATION TO BELIEVE

Those remarks bring us, then, to the second aspect of the scandal of the Christian witness: our witness is only an invitation, "Come and see." Notice that Philip does not engage Nathanael in discussion. He does not dispute with Nathanael the question of whether or not it is conceivable that the Prophet-Messiah should originate in Nazareth. He does not try to minimize that background nor try to explain it. Rather, he says simply, "Come and see." It is no accident that Philip is made here by our evangelist to repeat the words of Jesus to the first two disciples (v. 39).

"Come and see." Those words are the invitation to discover for oneself by belief. And how instructive that invitation is. It implies that the truth of the Christian witness cannot be discovered in passivity. The invitation, "Come and see," demands that the person act in order to discover. The truth for which Nathanael searches cannot be found in his passive consideration of Philip's arguments. Nathanael himself must act in order to know if there is anything that is good which can originate in Nazareth.

The scandal of the Christian witness today is that we are still required to act in order to know. There is no knowing of the Christian truth in passivity. We modern persons would rather quietly sit back, allow others to discover truth for us, and then present it to us. We would rather let the "experts" tell us what we should regard as truth and falsehood than investigate it for ourselves. During the U.S. involvement in Southeast Asia in the 1960s and early '70s, those opposed to that involvement continually asked the American people to investigate the facts and to decide for themselves the legality and morality of the war. But the response was continually that we must trust the experts; we must allow those who know about the situation to decide American policy in that troubled part of the world. Too many of us were for too long willing passively to allow others to discover the truth for us. As a consequence of our passivity, the war grew in tragic proportions until the opposition to it was vindicated.

Christian witness does not appeal to this passive willingness to believe what others have discovered to be true. It beckons us out of our passivity into action. And that action is the willingness to venture in faith. Faith is action! It is the risk of believing in order to discover. All the Christian witness can do is to invite that faith-act out of which the truth of the proclamation emerges. What Philip invites Nathanael to do is to venture an act of faith: "Come and see." The response to the offense of Jesus' humble origins is the summons to faith. The scandal cannot be minimized by argument or disputation. It can be confronted only in faith. "Only faith overcomes all objections and recognizes the divine origin of Jesus in spite of his earthly lowliness" (Rudolf Schnackenburg, *The Gospel According to St. John,* Vol. I, p. 315).

But the profound words, "Come and see," are even more than the summons to abandon passivity in a venture of faith. They are the assertion that Christian truth is found only in immediate experience. The witness of Philip cannot substitute for the firsthand experience of Nathanael with Jesus. Nathanael cannot be "sold" by hearing the convictions of Philip. He can only embrace this offensive Messiah out of his own experience with him.

We all know the limitations of secondhand experience. We can, for instance, read about the suffering of the Jewish people at the hands of anti-Semitism. We can listen intensely and empathetically to the tales of horror. But we stand even then at a distance from the experience itself. As powerful as they are, for instance, the writings of an Elie Wiesel still leave us Gentiles miles from the firsthand involvement in the Jewish experience. To know means finally to experience for ourselves, and until we have experienced for ourselves, all claims to truth are removed from the heart of our existence.

The import of Philip's luring of Nathanael is that the Christ truth is known only through firsthand experience. Nathanael responds to Philip's luring. He "comes and sees," and the result is his profession of faith: "Rabbi, you are the Son of God! You are the King of Israel!" (v. 49). But only his *own* experience could evoke that profession. Philip's role was only that of a signpost pointing Nathanael to where that kind of experience could be found. The scandal of our witness today is that we can be only signposts. We can be summoners and little more. To those who want to remain passive, to those who want the secondhand experience to suffice, we can only continue to point them to the Christ himself. Imagine trying to convince another of the beauty of a Beethoven symphony without that person's having ever heard the music performed. One can only say, "Come and hear it for yourself. Let the music convince you of its own beauty." Our Christian witness, as scandalous as it may seem, is only to try to lure the unbeliever into the first steps of the faith journey.

What the Christian witness contends, however, is that beyond the initial steps of that faith journey there lies the discovery of the truth of its proclamation. Truth is never known before the act of faith. We would like it otherwise. We would like to be able to present persuasive arguments and clinching evidence which would convince others of the truth of our position. The scene for Christian witness is not comparable to the courtroom. There in the courtroom the two sides of the case are presented thoroughly and carefully to the jury. The evidence is paraded before the attentive eyes and ears of those charged with determining the verdict. Passively they sit, weighing the arguments and the evidence of the two sides until they are persuaded by one or the other.

No, the scene is more comparable to an interpersonal relationship. You decide to engage in an intimate relationship of trust and sharing with another on the basis of firsthand experience which emerges from the gradual steps of a faithful trusting of the other. You do not gather all the evidence you can about the person; you do not interview everyone who has known this person; you do not investigate his or her background. You take the initial step of trusting the person. From that first venture of faith in the person you acquire an experience of her or him. On the basis of that experience you decide whether this person is trustworthy and capable of entering into a relationship of intimacy.

The scandal of the Christian witness is present, in part, in this fact: the truth of our position is known only beyond the initial step of faith. The taste of the food is known only after the first bite. As clumsy as it is, we must ask the uninitiated to take the leap of faith in order to know.

The scandal of Christian witness is vividly presented to us by John in this story of the calling of Nathanael. It is a two-edged offense: the humble origins of this one whom we claim to be God's decisive act in history for the salvation of humanity and the fact that we can only invite those who seek the truth to "Come and see."

We wish that we could make the appeal more attractive. If only we could decorate it with the polish and glitter of good sales techniques. But the way of God is not the way of the human, it would appear. His way is to require the venturous move of faith in the face of the most unbelievable of claims. The discomfort of the Christian witness is that it cannot be made without the presentation of the incredible, and it can appeal to faith alone as the way of knowing the truth of its declaration. "Can anything good come out of Nazareth?" "Come and see!"

Second Week:
The Scandal of Belief

John 2:12-22

The richness of our four gospels in the New Testament is due in part to the differences among them. Most especially the marked difference between John and the other three gospels enhances that richness. It is somewhat like the pleasures of enjoying steak and lobster on the same plate. Both are delicious, but their tastes are so very different. Enjoyed together they are a veritable taste sensation! Reading the synoptic gospels and the gospel of John provides the same sort of pleasure—both are inspiring, but both are so different. Taken together they are a veritable spiritual sensation.

THE CLEANSING OF THE TEMPLE IN JOHN

Our passage is John's version of the cleansing of the temple. Compared with the accounts in Matthew (21:12-13), Mark (11:15-17), and Luke (19:45-46), John's report of the incident is not so strikingly different. There are some differences, to be sure. Most important is the fact that John links with the cleansing of the temple a dialog between Jesus and the religious leaders (vv. 18-22). As we will notice shortly, the synoptics have reports of a similar kind of discussion but not associated immediately with the temple cleansing. But the glaring difference—indeed, the difference which adds to the richness of the gospel of John—is the location of the story of the temple cleansing in the ministry of Jesus. For the synoptic evangelists that incident is associated with the final days of Jesus' ministry; but for John it is an introduction to the ministry.

Let us not try to harmonize the two sequences. Such an effort is, in the long run, fruitless. Better to ask what John might have understood to be the meaning of this incident, standing as it does on the threshold of Jesus' ministry. Could it be that he is trying to tell us something about the significance of this event by placing it where he does in the life of Jesus? Certainly this much seems clear: for John this incident marks a kind of digest of what is to come in the future pages of his work. The author of a book today might very well lead off with a chapter that gives the reader the gist of what is to come. Or even in a novel the essential element in the weaving of the plot may appear subtly in the early pages. John is doing the same thing. In placing the temple cleansing where he does, he is letting his readers know that much of what follows involves the conflict of Jesus with the religious tradition of his time and his people. Jesus will challenge the religious establishment in the tradition of the great prophets of Israel; that is the meaning of the temple cleansing. The establishment will in turn confront Jesus and demand that he authenticate himself; that is the meaning of the discussion between Jesus and the religious leaders in verses 18-22 of our passage. These two elements—Jesus' prophetic action and the resistance of the religious establishment—are the tragic combination that will lead the central figure of the story to his death. John has skillfully allowed the reader a peek at the final conclusion of his story.

This leads us to make another kind of preparatory comment on our passage. You will note that the confrontation after the cleansing of the temple is with "the Jews" (v. 18). John is suggesting that the prophetic thrust of Jesus' ministry was toward a cleansing of Judaism. All of this has the ring of anti-Semitism to our modern ears. But we must be careful not to read John's view in that misfortunate context. John is telling us that the struggle of his own time (the struggle of his own church) was to work out the relationship between the Christian community and its faith and the Jewish community and its faith. There is much evidence that John's church was locked in a controversy with the Jewish synagogue of his community and that he was trying through the medium of his gospel to address that controversy. Hence, John calls the opponents of Jesus simply, "the Jews."

Where in the synoptic gospels we find Jesus having discussions with groups within the Judaism of his time and disagreeing with them (for example, the scribes and Pharisees), John calls these protagonists simply, "Jews." Compare, for example, John 2:18-22 with Matthew 21:23ff, Mark 11:27ff, and Luke 20:1ff. In all four Jesus' authority is challenged by a Jewish group. But in the synoptics it is "the chief priests and scribes and elders" who are the inquisitors, while in John they are called, "the Jews." It appears that John has lumped these religious leaders together under this one title. That he has done so suggests that his own conflict is with the Jewish leaders in general and that the distinctions among them is not relevant to him or his readers. In a community, for instance, where there is a group at odds with the city officials, it is easy for them to speak generally of "city hall." In point of fact, their opposition may be with more specific officials, say, the office of zoning; but they feel as if it is the entire institution of city government against which they must wage their battle. John's church is at odds with a specific synagogue and its leaders, but he writes as if the struggle is with "the Jews" in general. It behoves us then to see his comments not as a general indictment against the Jewish people and their religion but as a reflection of his own concrete situation.

THE REQUEST FOR A "SIGN"

But now into the heart of this passage and its message for us. Our attention must focus on John's insistence that the cleansing of the temple evoked an immediate response from the religious leaders and that Jesus replied to that response. The religious leaders inquired about the authority by which Jesus presumed to take such drastic action as he has done: "What sign have you to show us for doing this?" (v. 18). They ask for a sign to demonstrate to them Jesus' authority to act in this outlandish manner. Does he have the authorization to proclaim to them that their custom of having a mini-market in the temple area is a violation of the sanctity of the place of worship? Imagine if one came among your congregation some Sunday morning and declared that the taking of the offering was a defilement of the spirit of worship. Well, you would want to know who this person was. What right does he or she have to restrict your worship practices? Is this person a representative of the synodical office. A Ph.D. in worship? An officer from the Internal Revenue Service? "Show us your credentials," you would doubtless demand. The religious leaders are doing the same thing in our passage. They ask for a *sign*.

The word *sign* is a complicated one in the gospel of John. It is sometimes used in a disparaging way, as it is here. Father Raymond E. Brown suggests that at 2:18 the word means, "a miraculous, apologetic proof for unbelievers" (*The Gospel of John,* Vol. I, p. 115). But it is also used at times to describe the wonders of Jesus which reveal his true identity to those who are willing to believe (for example, 2:11 and 20:30). In general, we can say that the unsolicited works of Jesus which invite faith are legitimate signs, but that in the view of the Fourth Gospel, requests for signs are inappropriate and ill-motivated. Note that even in the story of the wonder at Cana Jesus refuses to do the sign simply at the request of his mother (2:4).

What the religious leaders are asking of Jesus is obviously some work of wonder which will convince them that Jesus has the right to purify the temple. Our passage suggests that the Messiah is not to be authenticated by miraculous signs. To their demand that Jesus show them proof that he has the right to tell them how the temple affairs should be conducted, he responds with an obscure reference which made no sense at all: "Destroy this temple and in three days I will raise it up" (v. 19). His opponents think that he is speaking of the temple building itself and are utterly dumbfounded. The temple had been under construction some 46 years and was not yet completed. How was this stranger going to rebuild it in three days? Verse 22 suggests that not even his disciples understood at the time what Jesus was saying.

Here is a perfect example of a common feature in the gospel of John. Again and again Jesus' words are entirely misunderstood by his hearers. We considered in an earlier chapter how puzzled Nicodemus was by Jesus' words regarding the rebirth from above. Nicodemus asks how it can be expected that an old man reenter his mother's womb to be brought forth a second time. We smile at Nicodemus' almost stupid misunderstanding of the words of Jesus. He interprets Jesus' words literally on the material plane, while Jesus is speaking symbolically on the spiritual plane. John represents the hearers of Jesus as continually doing just that: understanding his words on one level while Jesus intends them to refer to another level. It is a common error. The child is often confused by the way language is used to refer to the intangible. The little girl heard her daddy singing in the shower, "I left my heart in San Francisco." At her first opportunity she reproached her father for such a silly idea. "You can't leave your heart someplace, Daddy. It goes wherever you go." The hearers of Jesus are represented as childlike in their understanding of his words, constantly trying to force them into a materialistic frame of reference.

In this case the religious leaders suppose that Jesus is speaking of the physical temple. John, knowing that his readers might not catch Jesus' real meaning, tells us that Jesus is referring to the temple of his body and that the disciples understood this only after the resurrection. It is interesting that Jesus is here credited with these words. In Matthew and Mark it is reported that Jesus is charged with uttering a blasphemy against the temple by claiming that he was able to destroy the temple and rebuild it in three days (Matthew 26:61 and Mark 14:58). Matthew and Mark report this charge as coming from "false witnesses" at the trial of Jesus before the Jewish council (the Sanhedrin). It is startling to find nearly the same words reported in the gospel of John as an authentic utterance of Jesus, while the other gospels nowhere have him saying such a thing. John apparently knew the tradition that Jesus did speak such words, but that they were entirely misunderstood.

THE OFFENSE OF FAITH WITHOUT CERTAINTY

The refusal of Jesus to perform a *sign* to authorize himself and his actions suggests one of the scandalous features of our Christian faith and of Lent itself. The scandal is that Jesus asks us to believe him and accept his authority even though there is no sign which proves or gives certainty that he is who he says he is. Give the religious leaders the benefit of the doubt for a moment. Perhaps they would have been willing to grant Jesus the right to reform their faith if he had been able to document his authority. Theirs was in many respects a reasonable request. You want me to believe you? Then show me that you carry some authority. In these very pages when I make an assertion that such and such is the case, you want me to show you my authority for saying that it is the case. You want me to cite chapter and verse or to demonstrate that I have some background and basis on which to know that what I am saying is true. If I tell you, "Believe me without any such documentation," you are rightly offended. It is an *intellectual* offense to be asked to believe without proof. Had we been in the shoes of the religious leaders who witnessed the driving of the merchants and money-changers out of the temple, would we too not have wanted from Jesus the same sort of authorization? In the musical *Jesus Christ*

Superstar Jesus is brought before King Herod, and in one of the delightful lines of Herod's song, he asks Jesus to prove that he is the Messiah by walking across the palace swimming pool! We humans want some proof—some basis—if we are asked to believe.

Ah, but the offense is not just an intellectual one. It would be another matter entirely if it were. If it were just a matter of needing some evidence on which to base an intellectual idea, it might be possible to overcome this offense. If I said, "Show me the evidence that supports your theorem," it might be possible to accept the theorem even if there was no firm evidence for it. A claim to truth without adequate evidence is harmless if it is one of those about which we can truthfully say, "If that is so, so what? What difference does it make?"

But the offense of Jesus' asking us to believe him is an *existential* as well as an intellectual one. That is, it is a matter that is vitally important to us and our lives. Jesus is asking us to stake our lives on him. Here I stand with my meager 65 years or so of life that have been graciously extended to me, and this Jesus is saying, "Believe that I am who I say I am, but believe it without my presenting certain proof that my claim is true!" If I am asked to entrust my life's commitment in the hands of another, I want some firm indications that my trust is not being misplaced. It is like the fellow who fell off the cliff, but managed to catch hold of a tree protruding from the walls of the canyon and save himself the fatal fall to the rocks below. As he hung there helplessly, he called out, "Is there anyone up there who can help me?" A voice came out of the heavens: "Let go, and I'll catch you." The distraught fellow thought for a few seconds and again called out, "Is there anyone *else* up there who can save me?" We are not about to let go and trust someone to catch us unless we have been shown that he or she can be trusted.

Jesus, however, will not authenticate himself beyond doubt; he will not give us the kind of certainty that will make our faith in him easy. In another passage in John, Jesus is asked essentially the same question put to him in our passage: "What sign do you do, that we may see, and believe you?" (6:30). Just as he does in our passage, Jesus refused the request for a sign. He responds, but with still another claim for himself. (See the parallel story in Matt. 21:23-27, Mark 11:27-33, and Luke 20:1-8, as well as the similar incident found in Matt. 12:38-42, Mark 8:11-12, and Luke 11:29-32).

But isn't the resurrection of Christ a sign that he is indeed God's special anointed one? No, we cannot even appeal to that greatest marvel of marvels as grounds for our faith. Even the resurrection is an event which is at best ambiguous for the persons seeking proof that the Christian claims are true. To whom does the resurrected Christ appear, according to the New Testament? Not to those seeking signs on which to base their faith, but to those who already have dared to believe and follow him. To be sure, some of those had in the disturbing moments of the arrest, trial and execution fallen away and run like scared rabbits. But the appearance of the resurrected Christ had the effect of restoring their faltering faith; it was not the grounds of faith itself.

Futhermore, the resurrection did not and (even today) does not convince the uncommitted to believe. The New Testament is honest with us at this point. Matthew reports that some doubted even in the face of the experience of the resurrected Christ (28-17). And John includes in his gospel the account of Thomas' difficulties with the resurrection (20:24-29).

There is no act of Jesus recorded which offers to us unambiguous evidence that Jesus is truly the Christ. Not the resurrection. Not the miracles. We must conclude that the acts of Jesus are ambiguous—that is, open to interpretation. A poor parallel, but perhaps helpful nonetheless, is available to us in the reports of scientific research. One group of scholars runs an experiment and interprets the evidence in one way; but they are challenged by other groups of scientists who show that the evidence resulting from the experiment might be interpreted differently to produce entirely different conclusions. The ambiguity of our language, too, is suggestive of the ambiguity of the reported acts of Jesus. "You look like a million dollars!" may be interpreted to mean that we are looking healthy and vigorous. Or, the same comment may be taken to mean that we look wrinkled and green! The response to Jesus' acts is similar: either he is what he says he is, or else he is a deranged fanatic. Either he is the Christ (Mark 8:29), or else he is a representative, not of God, but of Satan (Mark 3:22).

The terrifying result is that we must believe without the benefit of certainty. Or, to put it in a positive way, we are left to believe only on faith. Rudolf Bultman put it well: "Jesus refused to give a sign in proof of his authority, such as would enable men to recognize him without risk, without committing themselves to him" (*The Gospel According to John, p.* 125). The scandal of Lent is that belief in this Christ is a risk of faith without certainty. Why is it so? Perhaps because belief in Christ must be full commitment. It must be an either-or situation. Were there absolute certainty for our religious faith, our commitments would be shallow. If a team of scientists demonstrated the strength of a chair for you, so that it is unquestionably true that it will sustain your weight, you make no personal commitment when you sit down in that chair. You are not trusting the chair; the necessity of trust has been eliminated, for the most part. Our Christian faith is a trusting commitment of ourselves which involves response from every fiber of our being. That we must believe without certainty necessitates that we believe either with our whole persons or not at all.

The scandal of Lent includes the offense, then, of being asked to trust fully this person Jesus in spite of the fact that there is no certainty that our trust is well placed. It is like the risk the swimmer must take. He has no certainty that the water will sustain his body. He has heard those claims made, but he cannot know them to be true or false until he trusts the water. He enters the water without absolute certainty and takes the risk of being pulled under by the water. Or, the parachutist trains all she can. She jumps from a platform and learns to fall correctly. She tests a chute from a still higher platform. But until she takes that first jump from miles above the earth she cannot have the personal sense of security that her chute will bring her gently down to earth.

In other words, Christ is a Messiah who is known only in faith. He is known only by surrendering the security of certainty in the risk of faith. And to our scientifically oriented minds, that is offensive. We are a people trained to look for scientific proof even before we trust our teeth to a particular brand of toothpaste or our headaches to a brand of aspirin. We are now asked to trust this Savior—to trust him with our whole lives—before we have certainty about him. That is the scandal of belief in the gospel of John. But more, that is the scandal of Christian faith and especially the scandal we face this Lenten season.

Third Week:
The Scandal of Sensuality

John 6:53-58

American culture has become bogged down in the theme of sensuality. Not too many years ago we had a rash of books concerned with the rediscovery of human sensuality, particularly in the realm of sexuality. First, there was *The Sensuous Woman,* followed soon by *The Sensuous Man.* Then, we got the two of them together in *The Sensuous Couple.* We even topped it off with a book entitled, *The Sensuous Christian.* After years of repressing sexual impulses, it appears that we have rediscovered sexual sensuality, and like children with a new toy we seem obsessed with it. New forms of psychotherapy encourage us to explore the bodily senses. The realm of the physical body is like a new frontier to be explored and—unfortunately, like most new frontiers—exploited.

But there is a valuable truth in this movement which encourages us to find new meaning in the bodily senses. We have been too long inclined to hold the bodily and sensual in reserve —to view them with some suspicion. They have become associated with the realm of the sinful. For whatever reason such attitudes may have developed in the past, the present movement awakes us to the positive side of human sensuality and invites us to rethink that part of our creation. As persons who see the serious dangers inherent in the careless driving of an automobile might declare automobiles sinful and refuse to ride or drive one, we have seen the destructive potential of human sensuality and for that reason declared it evil. It is time our narrow vision in this matter be corrected.

THE OFFENSIVENESS OF JESUS' CLAIMS

If we are willing to regard the sensual as a gift of God's gracious creation, our eyes are opened to a theme in the gospel of John. That theme is nowhere more vividly expressed than in the passage which is the subject for our reflection in this chapter.

Chapter 6 of the gospel of John is an extraordinary piece. It begins with John's version of the feeding of the multitude—a story we find recorded for us in each of our gospels (Matt. 14:13-21, Mark 6:32-44 and 8:1-10, and Luke 9:10-17). Then follows the wonder of Jesus' walking on the water (again a story familiar to us from the other gospels—Matt. 14:22-27 and Mark 6:45-52). But next comes Jesus' encounter once again with some of the crowd who had benefited from his marvelous feeding and a dialog ensues from that encounter (vv. 25-34). Jesus then launches into what has been called the discourse on the bread of life, which runs on through verse 59, to be followed by a report of the results of his words in verses 60-71. The chapter begins with a marvelous act of the feeding of the crowd and their effort to declare him king (v. 15); but it ends, after the long discourse concerning the bread of life, with many of his followers turning away from him, unable to believe the claims he has made for himself (vv. 66-71). The drama of the chapter moves then from the heights of enthusiasm to the depths of unbelief. And between are the scandalous claims which Jesus makes for himself.

The long teaching section of the chapter is divided into several clear parts. Verses 25-34 serve as a kind of introduction to the themes of the discourse. In verses 35-50 Jesus discusses his person; he is the bread of life in the sense of the revelation of God. Verses 51-59 reiterate those words of verses 35-50 with a sharper emphasis upon the bodily symbolism.

I have taken care to show you the structure of this chapter in a brief way because it is important to understand that the passage on which we will focus our attention stands in a context in the gospel of John. It appears that the evangelist has constructed this chapter in large part out of his concern to show the meaning of Jesus' act of feeding the crowd with the loaves and fishes. Typically, John narrates the story of the feeding and then has a discourse which elucidates the significance of the act just completed. That is the way John seems consciously to have brought the materials at his disposal into a gospel form—narration followed by Jesus' explanatory words on the event. (For an additional example, see Chapter 5). John would not want us, therefore, to examine 6:53-58 without understanding it as one part of a larger speech of Jesus which in turn is tied to an act by Jesus, in this case the feeding of the crowd.

The words of Jesus in verses 53-58 are words which evoked disbelief and even indignation. John tells us, "Many of his disciples, when they heard it [verses 53-58], said, 'This is a hard saying; who can listen to it?'" (v. 60). The disciples are scandalized by the words this teacher of theirs has just spoken. And it is not just the crowd or the religious leaders who take offense at these words; John calls them, "disciples." They are those who had up to this point pledged their allegiance to Jesus, followed him, listened to him, and respected him. Now, however, he has gone too far. They are unable to stretch their faith in him far enough to accept these radical words.

What are these words which so upset some of the disciples that they change their minds entirely about Jesus? What is so offensive about them? The breaking point, according to John, for these followers of Jesus seems to be the claim of Jesus that his flesh and blood are essential spiritual sustenance. "Unless you eat the flesh of the Son of man and drink his blood, you have no life in you. . . . For my flesh is food indeed, and my blood

43

is drink indeed. He who eats my flesh and drinks my blood abides in me, and I in him" (vv. 53 and 55-56).

If we take the response of disbelief in its broadest context in the chapter, we see the reason for the reaction quite clearly. These sometime followers of Jesus are offended by the idea that the sustaining bread from heaven should be focused in the life of one man. In other words, the offense which comes to expression here is really *the offense of the incarnation!* That the essential message of God—which alone leads humans to the proper understanding of God, themselves, and the world—is now to be found in the life of one individual is ridiculous on the face of it. How can the eternal truths of reality find their total expression in one human life confined to space and time? Behind the incredulity of the disciples in v. 60 stands a more fundamental unwillingness to believe the Christian message because of its claim that revelation occurs in a historical person. It seems that what we have before us is an instance of what John warned us about in the prologue of his gospel: "He [the incarnate Word of God] came to his own home, and his own people received him not" (1:11).

REVELATION THROUGH ONE HUMAN PERSON

If the fundamental scandal here is the idea that God should reveal himself in one human person, it is easy for us to feel some sympathy for those disciples who found it hard to listen to this kind of talk. There is in us all a propensity to feel a bit uneasy with the thought that the bread of life which God extends to us is found in one human life, lived some two thousand years ago. This is offensive to us, for we cannot conceive of the eternal being contained within the temporal; we cannot grasp the possibility of the infinite taking abode in the finite; we cannot comprehend the ultimate being focused in a contingent being.

But behind the offense we feel there is also the assumption that there is something dirty and unbecoming about concrete humanity. We can speak highly of the "human spirit," but when it comes to affirming the totality of the human—flesh and blood as well as spirit—we become nervous. It is like the thought of serving the president of the United States a TV dinner in our kitchen with the dirty dishes still in the sink. God ought not to soil his divinity with the human person. We have in us an inclination similar to one which brought the heresy in the early church called *doceticism* (from the Greek word meaning, "to appear"). These Christians were so convinced that the material, fleshly world was evil, as opposed to the divine and spiritual world, that they could not accept the idea of God's revealing himself as a human being embodied in flesh. Instead, they preferred to think that Jesus only *appeared* to have a human body. Actually, he was pure, unadulterated spirit floating a few inches off the ground and tricking everyone into thinking that he was a real human person. Our instincts lead us in that same direction. Surely God did not incarnate himself in a real human body! Surely Jesus was not really—not flesh and blood—human the way we are. That would be like sending a bride in her white dress into a coal mine!

I encountered this kind of reluctance to believe that Jesus was actually and fully a human (in what I like to call a flesh and blood way) in classes of college-age young people in the early 1970s. Even among these young adults, who were generally considered by the standards of the day to be wildly liberal and iconoclastic, there was a tendency to think of Jesus as moving above the basic human instincts. The occasion for this discovery was the study and discussion of Nikos Kazantzakis' novel, *The Last Temptation of Christ*. In this provocative and imaginative telling of the story of Jesus' passion, the Greek novelist attributes to Jesus the basic sexual drives known to all humans. Kazantzakis never goes so far as to suggest that Jesus attempted to fulfill his sexual drives and even treats them in the noblest of ways (for example, Jesus' yearnings to have a family). And yet the very idea that Jesus' humanity might be so complete as to include the sexual dimension of human existence deeply offended the sensibilities of many of these young

45

people (indeed as it may offend yours). The point is not to argue whether Kazantzakis is correct in his view of the Christ figure but to point out the often unspoken desire on the part of many of us to avoid the scandalous idea that this Master of ours was a *real* man. It is to bring us face to face with the claim of the gospel of John that God actually became flesh with all that that entails.

The scandal of the incarnation is basically an offense to our concept of the human and in particular the fleshly dimension of humanity. We are still victims, it seems to me, of the idea that the body and the spirit of humans are really two incompatibles dwelling temporarily together. This idea—one which goes far back into the thought of western civilization and has roots perhaps in Greek philosophy—contends that the human spirit is captured within the prison of the physical body. The spirit is good and pure and noble, but it is held in chains to the passions of the physical body, which is evil and corrupt. This splits the human into two parts—one good and one evil.

But such a division of body and spirit is foreign to the biblical way of conceiving of the human. That difference is most noticeable in the Old Testament where the ancient Hebrews affirmed the absolute unity of the human person. They could never conceive of the human, for instance, existing without a physical body. And so, when they finally began to think in terms of a life beyond the grave, they thought of it not in terms of the survival of the soul of the human after the body had been separated and laid to rest, but of the resurrection of the body. The flavor of this point of view is that the physical body is fundamentally good (see Gen. 1:31), so that God could honor it in a resurrection from the grave. This view is continued through most of the New Testament (see, for instance, 1 Corinthians 15).

The perspective of the fourth evangelist is solidly Hebraic in this regard. Because his view of the physical body is not that the body is somehow tainted and evil, he could affirm with all of its implications that the bread of heaven was now incarnated in the flesh and blood life of Jesus of Nazareth. He could say that unless that specific human person is taken into our lives, ingested like the food that nourishes our bodies, we can have none of the spiritual nourishment we so desperately need. And John makes this as sharp as possible. He employs the clearest word in Greek he has to refer to the flesh of Jesus, *sarx*. There was another word at his disposal—*soma*. But *soma* had the sense of the total person, physical and spiritual. And it is this latter word which is used in the accounts of the Last Supper in which Jesus says, "This is my body [*soma*] which is for you" (1 Cor. 11:24). So he chose the word which more clearly indicated his conviction that the bodily life of Jesus (his flesh and blood) was the source of our knowledge of God's truth for us. There is an implication in John's words which is offensive to us—that normal bodily life of human beings is the proper dwelling place for the bread from heaven.

Let us admit it. Many of us too would have fallen away had we heard this man Jesus speak of his flesh and blood as the manna from heaven. That is offensive to us. We would rather not have to think of it in that way.

A brief parenthesis in our discussion is demanded at this point. The words of the Johannine Jesus at 6:63 would seem to contradict some of what has just been said, for there Jesus states, "It is the spirit that gives life, the flesh is of no avail." Do not these words sound as if John is invoking a division of flesh and spirit and denigrating the fleshly? Actually, however, the context is different, and the point is different. What John has Jesus say at this juncture we might paraphrase with these words: "It is the divine—it is God alone—who gives life in its fullest sense, and one cannot gain this life with human powers." The point is similar to that found in 3:3 and 8, where the new birth is the work of the Spirit of God, not human efforts. 6:63 should not, therefore, be taken as a relegation of the bodily flesh to the realm of evil. It is an affirmation of the power of the divine as opposed to the impotence of the human.

REVELATION THROUGH PHYSICAL SENSES

John presents his scandalous truth in a still wider dimension. This report of his that Jesus claimed his flesh and blood to be the revelation of God only epitomizes a more fundamental view of the Fourth Gospel. John not only declares to us that the Word became concrete and specific flesh in the person of Jesus, he also claims that the truth of God is known to us humans precisely through the use of the senses.

How does he do this? First, he does it by suggesting that the acts of Jesus are in actuality *signs*. That is, they are concrete, historical deeds which must be perceived first on a basic sensory level and then on the more profound level of their meaning. We must witness the deed of Jesus ("see" it) and then on the basis of what we have witnessed draw conclusions. This latter step—drawing conclusions from what we have witnessed—is where for John belief is born. There are a number of these acts of Jesus which John specifically calls *signs,* for instance the wonder done at the wedding in Cana (2:1-11). But his statement in 20:30 leads us to believe that he understood all of the acts of Jesus as potential signs: "Now Jesus did many other signs in the presence of the disciples, which are not written in this book." In other words, the physically perceptible acts of Jesus are the means by which we are led to faith.

But more startling is his use of the words, "seeing" and "hearing." In any number of passages (e.g., 3:32) John suggests that the door to faith is the sensory experiences of seeing and hearing. If one sees Jesus, she or he sees the Father (14:9); if one hears Jesus, she or he hears the Father (8:25-27). The point is that the experience of encounter with God is found within the sensory experiences of Jesus. The senses are the conveyors of truth—divine truth.

This may not seem, on the surface at least, to be a terribly profound assertion. But wait and consider for a moment what the evangelist is telling us. He is saying that our access to the divine truth is through our physical, bodily senses. He is telling us that sight, sound, taste, and touch are the means by which we come to know God's truth. Is it not the case that we would think just the opposite? Would we not want to say that the secret of knowing God is not to attend to the physical senses at all but rather to some additional sense—let's call it a spiritual sense? Indeed, we might even want to say that one must ignore one's physical senses, if one is to know the divine truth. Implied in the practices of meditation imported into our culture from the Asian and Indian religions is the basic assumption that one comes in touch with the divine through a conquest over the physical. In meditation one is asked to think beyond the sensual responses of the body—even when it is tied up in the lotus position—to the realm of the higher consciousness, where God may be encountered. Asked to choose, most of us would say that we know God's presence through a sense other than those of touch, sight, sound, and taste. To become too preoccupied with those sensations is to miss the capacity of the human spirit (not the body) to communicate with God.

But here is our evangelist telling us not only that the flesh and blood of Jesus is the bread from heaven but telling us further that divine truth comes to us through our capacity to see and hear. Ah, but did he mean that only for those so privileged as to be able to see and hear and touch the man, Jesus of Nazareth? Does John mean that those who were firsthand witnesses to God's incarnation could by means of their sensory experiences with Jesus come to know God's truth, while those of us living in other times and places must resort to "spiritual" means of knowing? To interpret John in that way is more comfortable for us. Indeed, it allows us to keep our preconceptions intact and to continue our convenient separation of the physical and the spiritual.

But this John was a thorough incarnationalist. He had a fundamental view of how God communicated with humans which would lead him to believe that anyone in any time and place knows God through the sensory experiences. He is not saying that it is only the sensory experiences of the historical Jesus of

Nazareth which are revelatory for us. He is saying much more. He is saying that God is always known to humans through how they interpret the sensory experiences of their everyday lives.

Let me use an illustration of what I mean and what I think John is driving at. There was once a man who had become fully convinced that God was dead. There was for this person no sense of the presence of God whatsoever. He had tried all of the ways to know God that he could. He had prayed, meditated, read the Scriptures, gone to church, and all the rest. But he was met by utter silence. The cosmos, instead of being inhabited by a God who sought relationships with humans, was cold, silent, and deaf. He had tried to nurture the "spiritual" dimension of his life, but had finally admitted to himself that he had no sense at all of what the spiritual was. He became a totally discouraged, pessimistic, and defeated man.

But then he met a young woman who, for reasons only she could explain, came to love this man very deeply. At first, he resisted her love, for he felt that love too must be a mere figment of the human imagination, along with God, the spiritual realm, and all the rest. But as her love persisted, he responded, slowly at first and then eventually wholeheartedly. He experienced the sensations of her love. Her love for him was conveyed in the way she looked at him, in her touch, in the taste of her kisses, in the sound of her words of concern. The sensual experiences of love made him aware of her love for him. But they did something else for him. Strangely, because of these experiences of love, he came to feel that he was being loved not only by this woman but by God. The sensual experiences of touch, sight, sound, and taste were the means by which he came to reflect on the meaning of her love for him. And he found that behind her love—coming through her love for him—was a cosmic love: the love of God. Their relationship was for him a sacrament—a means by which he received the grace of God. That love of the woman and of God through the love of the woman transformed his life. He found God, or God found him. And it occurred not by his ignoring or rising above the physical senses but through those senses. What he experienced sensually he began to interpret; he tried to understand the meaning of those sensory experiences, and in that exploration of meaning he found God waiting to be known. The story I tell here is a true one, for it is my own story.

What John may be telling us, as scandalous as it may sound, is that God is to be found lurking behind the sensory experiences of our daily lives. Those sensations are our threshold to the eternal. Shocking, isn't it? The finite is the door to the infinite. The temporal is the pathway to the eternal. The human is the entrance to the divine. That may offend us, accustomed as we are in driving such a sizable wedge between those two realms of reality. But John declares that the divine message for us is found quite literally at our fingertips.

But John is only really recalling us to a basic tenet of the biblical faith. The Old Testament is built upon the bold faith that the actions and the revelations of God could be found within the compass of human history itself. A people suffers in slavery in Egypt and is led out of that slavery into freedom at the hand of a prophet named Moses. But Israel claimed that this event in human history in which a handful of oppressed people gained their freedom is actually the act of God himself. A people suffers in exile away from their homeland, lost and depressed. Their conquerors are themselves conquered by another empire, and their new rulers declare that the people are free to return to their homeland, occupy it, and rebuild it. A mere paragraph in the chronicle of human history? Not for the Israelites. They saw in that event once again the hand of God saving them from their plight. The sense of the Hebraic faith is that what one witnesses on the plane of human history is the data from which one learns through interpretation the reality and will of the Creator and Sustainer of the universe. It is what one sees and hears, touches and tastes, on the human, physical plane which informs one of the divine plane.

What shall we do with such scandalous ideas as we have

discovered here in the gospel of John and most especially in 6:53-58? We may disregard them—or claim that they are distorted understandings of the gospel. But are they not essentially what the church has been inviting us for centuries to believe? As we share the sacrament of the Eucharist, touching and tasting these material objects of bread and wine, we are asked to experience the real presence of the divine Revealer. In the sight and touch of the water of Holy Baptism we are told we find the cleansing love of God. Is the church not inviting us to live our daily lives sensitive to the reality of God behind, under, and around the material realities which make up our lives? Is the scandal of sensuality which we found in the gospel of John not really the same as the scandal of sacramentality? Is it not just as offensive to the human mind to claim that bread and wine are the real presence of Christ and that the water of Baptism the bathing of God as it is to claim that God incarnates himself in our world in persons and events?

The scandal of sensuality is that God has chosen to make himself accessible to us in this real world where we live and work. He does not beckon us to leave this material world for some spiritual world before we may confront him. No, he is awaiting us "at the other end" of our sensory experiences, inviting us to understand these sensory experiences of ours as possible lines of communication with him.

"This is a hard saying; who can listen to it?" But if we can not only listen but *hear*, we may find that for which we most eagerly yearn.

Fourth Week:
The Scandal of
Heaven on Earth

John 5:21-27

As I am writing these lines, the world is filled with tension. At the dawn of the decade of the 1980s there are crises in several places in the world. The threat of world war looms larger than it has for many years. At the same time, the news is filled with one tragedy after another—world hunger and starvation, inflation, assassinations, and so on. By the time you read these lines, the crises I have in mind may have been resolved. But realism, and not necessarily skepticism, dictates that our world will be facing new crises of equal if not larger proportions. Time marches on—but increasingly one gets the feeling that it marches on from one crisis to another.

The only things which distract from the crises of world dimension are the personal crises in our individual lives. It may be the death of a loved one, illness, accidents, broken relationships within the family, economic woes, or personal alienation. Again, the list could go on and on. Our lives are woven with the ever-recurring threads of difficulty and suffering. From birth to death the personal journey is one which passes through the troubled waters of suffering (physical and mental) and the valleys of the shadow of death.

How startling it is, then, to hear in the gospel of John that one who believes in Christ already has eternal life! How odd that Jesus should claim through this gospel that Christian faith is the experience of heaven on earth. Tell me that during one of my several personal tragedies or in the midst of agonizing over a threatening world crisis, and you might well receive a rejoinder such as, "Nonsense" or "Rubbish!" Life seldom seems like a heaven on earth; and, when it does, we know that it is a passing moment moving steadily toward another experience of suffering. John's gospel brings us up short with its claims for the present reality of the blessings God has promised. It confronts our realism with an apparent contradiction which smacks of a dream-like idealism. What's this gospel trying to tell us with passages such as the one taken as a theme for this chapter?

THE CHRISTIAN HOPE IN JOHN

First of all, let's survey the teaching of the gospel of John with regard to the so-called eschatological blessings—that is, those hopes given to the Christian for the final days. In several places throughout the gospel, John has Jesus speak as if the blessings of the final days are present realities for those who respond to Christ in faith. 5:24 claims that the believer *has* eternal life. The same claim is made in 3:36. The believer is already resurrected from the grips of death, Jesus says, in 5:21, 24, 26. His claim that he *is* the resurrection in 11:25 implies that one bound to him in faith has already experienced resurrection. Furthermore, the Fourth Gospel presents us with a view of judgment which suggests that one is judged already in this life and not the next life (or at the end of history). 3:18, 5:24, and 9:39 are among the passages which most clearly express that point of view. Finally, even the defeat of the "ruler of this age" is said to have already occurred (12:31). Now what is surprising about all of this is that John has Jesus speak as if these future and hoped-for blessings are already experiences of the Christian believer. What other portions of the New Testament would seem to have us look for at the end of the course of human history, John invites us to look for in our present experience.

In fairness we must point out that the gospel of John is not consistent on this point. While the passages we have cited speak of the eschatological blessings as present experiences, there are other passages in which the blessings are assigned their place at the end of the age. Judgment is a future phenomenon in 12:48, as is eternal life (12:25), resurrection (6:39-40, 54), and the second appearing of Christ (14:3, 18, 28). Scholars have labored almost endlessly with this apparent contradiction. The results of such labors are a number of different explanations. Our interests are not in those explanations, but in the general consensus that, for whatever reason, the fourth evangelist stressed to a remarkable degree the present reality of the blessings which are usually assigned to the end of the course of human history.

Whatever his inclination to state the hope of Christians for eternal life, resurrection, and judgment beyond the scope of this life, he wounds our sense of realism about life with his frequent insistence that Christians are living the blessings of the final days. That is an offense to our lived reality of suffering and hardship. Can we pursue this scandal to find some sense in it—even if it is a sense which contradicts our perception of reality?

Our pursuit of this scandal of "heaven on earth" has several avenues, each of which needs to be travelled before we stand squarely before the offensive claims of the Johannine Christ. The first is the avenue of "eternal life."

ETERNAL LIFE

A hasty count will demonstrate that this expression, "eternal life," is one of the favorites of John. Of the approximately 44 occurrences in the New Testament, 23 uses of "eternal life" are found in Johannine literature—17 in the gospel and 6 in the Johannine epistles. We are dealing, then, with a central Johannine idea—one which the evangelist found most useful in articulating his message. In general when John employs this phrase, "eternal life," he is making one of two points: Christ is the source of eternal life (4:14, 36; 6:27; 10:28; 12:50; 17:2-3) or the believer has eternal life (3:15-16; 5:24, 39; 6:40, 47, 54, 68; 12:25). His message is then quite simple: in Christ one has access to eternal life through a faithful response.

But what did he mean by the expression? Popular Christian thought takes it to refer to life beyond the grave, a life unbounded by time or termination. The weakness of this popular conception is that eternal life is understood as a state or condition which awaits the believer beyond the experience of death. Before we can come to grips with the message of the Fourth Gospel, we must adjust this popular point of view. For the fourth evangelist, eternal life is quite clearly an experience of this life and not exclusively one beyond the pale of death. Jesus claims, "One who hears my word and believes him who sent me, *has* eternal life." The sense of those words is that the believer knows the experience of eternal life now—in this world, in this life. If John had meant for us to understand that the believer has the *promise* of eternal life firmly in hand, he would surely have said just that. No, John seems to mean exactly what he has Jesus say: the believer *has* eternal life.

What can that mean? Especially what can that mean given the fact of human suffering and tragedy? Our quest for the answer to those questions is helped by looking at how John employs the word, "life." There are occasional uses of this word in the gospel which we might take to mean simply "existence" (e.g., 10:11, 15, 17-18). But there are more frequent occurrences of the word which suggest that the fourth evangelist does not intend for us to think of existence as the synonym for life. Look at the use of the word throughout Chapter 6, especially in the claim of Jesus, "I am the bread of life" (vv. 35, 48). Or, again the verse in the prologue, "In him was life, and the life was the light of men" (1:4). And the clincher seems to be 10:10, where John has Jesus say that he came to give life, and then, as if to clarify what he means, adds, "and have it abundantly."

The common uses of the word, "life," and the expression, "eternal life," seem to be the fourth evangelist's way of referring to a *quality* of existence, not merely existence itself. It appears that these are terms John would have us take to mean his way of expressing what others might call "salvation." In other words, *eternal life (or simply life) means the kind of existence possible for humans who have by faith comprehended their true identity and who live in a relationship of love with their Creator.* Eternal life is a quality of life which begins in this worldly existence when persons are brought to a realization of their true being, and it continues unbroken beyond the experience of death.

Such a conception of eternal life ought not to be difficult for us to grasp. We know well that there are distinctions among the qualities of life. The advances of modern medicine have brought us face to face with the question of what constitutes life. The courts and the medical professions struggle with the definition of life. Is a person alive when there are no signs of activity in the brain? Is a person alive when his or her breathing is done only with the help of external machinery? Is a person alive when she or he has existed for months in a comatose state? But we have long recognized that life is more than breathing and thinking. We speak of the "walking dead." We know persons who seem only to exist from one day to another without any sense of emotion or even thought. And now common parlance has given birth to the expression, "the quality of life."

John is telling us that the quality of life for which human existence is intended is found in a faithful response to Christ. That quality of life is eternal life—not necessarily because it is without termination (although John surely teaches that), but because it is life which most completely realizes the potential of human existence. And John is boldly declaring that that quality of life can be embraced even amid the sufferings and the tragedies of this world. He never claims that those tragic realities of life are eliminated or even minimized. Rather, he seems to suggest that one lives the quality of life called eternal amid the dimension of the afflictions of this world. Indeed, to the same disciples to whom Jesus has said, "One who hears my word and believes in me has eternal life," he later says, "In the world you have tribulation" (16:33). Eternal life is the faith posture which allows us, even amid tribulation, to "be of good cheer," because we know Christ has "overcome the world."

This point is an important one. If Christians suppose that faith shields them from the tragedies of life, they have, of course, misunderstood the character of Christian life. The heaven on earth promised to those who would believe and hence have eternal life is not an existence free of suffering. It is one, instead, empowered to live through the suffering. A long-distance runner trains vigorously over a long period of time preparing his or her body for the race. With all of the training, however, the runner is not insured against the pain of enduring the race. The assurance is that the training will have produced such strength in the body that the pain can be endured. Embracing the eternal life offered to us in Christ does not insure us against the pains of life, but it does assure us that there will be the strength available to endure those pains.

As difficult as it may be for us to comprehend, particularly at times of suffering, faith in Christ yields the possibility of knowing eternal life even in this world. Heaven is on earth insofar as we are by faith enabled to grasp the deepest meaning and significance of life.

RESURRECTION

It is now time to explore another of the avenues leading in the direction of John's offensive claim that the blessings of the future are available to the Christian in the present. Verse 21 claims that Christ raises from the dead those to whom he chooses to give this life: "For as the Father raises the dead and gives them life, so also the Son gives life to whom he will." And

58

those who have been given eternal life have "passed from death to life" (v. 24). *Resurrection is a present reality in the life of the Christian.*

Indeed, the richness of the scene in 11:20-27 makes this point dramatically. Jesus has arrived too late on the scene. His friend, Lazarus, is already dead. Martha hears Jesus coming and rushes out to meet him. In a statement of faith (with only half understanding) Martha says, "Lord, if you had been here, my brother would not have died. And even now I know that whatever you ask from God, God will give you." Jesus then boldly announces to her, "Your brother will rise again." You can almost hear the meaninglessness in the words of Martha: "I know that he will rise again in the resurrection at the last day." Martha knows that and indeed believes it; but it is little consolation to her at the moment. Then Jesus confronts her with the truth she has only dimly glimpsed: *"I am* the resurrection and the life; he who believes in me, though he die, yet shall he live, and whoever lives and believes in me shall never die." With that Jesus proceeds to demonstrate the truth of his words: Lazarus is raised from his tomb.

Resurrection is experienced when one is bonded to Christ in faith. I doubt that John wanted necessarily to deny the truth of the promise of the resurrection from the dead at the last day (see 6:39-40, 54). Rather, I think he wanted to express vividly and forcefully the experience of resurrection in this life when one ingests the quality of life offered in Christ.

The symbols of death and resurrection are used almost glibly in some Christian circles today. But I think John is doing more than using the resurrection *symbol* to speak of the birth of faith. It seems more likely that he is saying that the real resurrection is not the one which raises us from the confines of our tombs to immortal life with God. It is, rather, the drastic reorientation of the person which takes place with the appropriation of God's gift to us in Christ ("I am the resurrection and the life"). My point is simply to suggest that John does not mean that the appropriation of life in Christ is *like* a resurrection. It is *the* resurrection itself.

For John, then, the apprehension of that eternal life is a rising from death. To grasp life as it is intended is to be rescued from an existence which is little more than death. Let me strike an analogy which is only feebly effective: the child is resurrected from the darkness of a toneless world the minute she begins playing the rudimentary scales on the piano. When as an accomplished pianist she performs a concerto with a full orchestra before a packed audience, she reaps the fruits of her life with the instrument. But the initial act of entering that world of music marks the real resurrection of her true musicianship. John may be suggesting the fact that Christians are resurrected to their true personhood in the initial act of faith and that the resurrection from physical death is but the eventual fruit of that initial act.

Again, John shocks us. He turns our minds around. Focus your view not on that future resurrection from the physical tomb but on the transformation which takes place in the faith response to Christ. We should not so much yearn for the future resurrection as appreciate the resurrection we have experienced in the birth of our faith relationship with Christ.

But living in these frail and aging bodies of ours and suffering the failure of spirit again and again in the course of life's trials, it is hard for us to know ourselves as resurrected persons —persons to whom life has already been given and given in abundance. It is scandalous to us that John would have us view that initial act of embracing Christ as our resurrection. It is much easier for us to say *no* to ourselves as we are in our Christian lives and to look for a more fundamental renewal beyond death. But John keeps insisting that we look to the present, to the *nows* of our daily life. Heaven is on earth; heaven is now. But you cannot appreciate it if your vision is focused only on the future. But we are ahead of ourselves. We must travel still another avenue before we come to the destination that the fourth evangelist has in mind for us.

JUDGMENT

That last avenue is the one of judgment. The one who hears and believes Jesus has eternal life, is resurrected, and "does not come into judgment" (5:24). John presents us with still another mind-boggling concept in his treatment of the theme of judgment. The scandalous suggestion of this unusual gospel is that humans judge themselves. Another passage in John expresses this idea more fully than does the one we have under consideration. "He who believes in him is not condemned; he who does not believe is condemned already, because he has not believed in the name of the only Son of God" (3:18). (Actually the Greek word in this passage translated, "condemned," is the word for the act of passing a judgment.) The general theme which runs throughout the gospel is that we pronounce our own judgment in terms of how we respond to Christ. The offer of life in Christ is the occasion for the trial, and the verdict is very simply in whether or not we accept that offer of life.

This is an offensive idea from the very start. We are accustomed to think that it is God who is our judge. It is he who offers the verdict on our lives. But now we hear John suggesting that it is we ourselves who are the judges. The judgment is contained within the act of our saying *yes* or *no* to Christ. Suddenly the responsibility is thrust back on us. It is safer, more comfortable even, to think that it is God who pronounces judgment on us than it is to accept the burden of the responsibility of being our own judges. The demonic implication which has crept into our lives with the advent of modern psychology is that we are always the products of our environment and we do not bear the responsibility for our own actions. A teen-ager plagued with a record of behavior that was destructive to her life glibly excused her actions on the basis of her background. "My parents did not discipline me as they should have when I was a child." Her counselor then had to force the girl to take up responsibility for her own life. So long as she could pass that responsibility off onto her parents, she could never make the decisions which would redirect her life along more constructive paths. John, like that counselor, is forcing us to take responsibility for our lives by his insistence that we are our own judges.

Rudolf Bultmann has argued that the act of God in Christ places humans in question. Confronted with the offer of God in Christ, we are forced to ask the fundamental questions of ourselves: Who are we? What are we for? What is our destiny in this world? What is our origin? What is the intention for our lives? John has this in mind when he suggests that it is we ourselves who are the judges. Christ puts us into question.

An excursus at this point—brief although it must be—might prove helpful. The Greek word translated, "judgment," is a rich word. In transliteration it is *krisis,* and from it comes the English word, *crisis.* Judgment is a crisis, and it is also a decision. It is a moment in our experience when we must make a critical decision, the consequences of which will be judgmental. A confrontation with Christ is a crisis. It is a critical moment in which we must make a decision. That decision—to believe this man or not to believe him—judges us.

The truth of this is evident in our lives. When one person expresses love for another, the second is placed in a life-questioning and critical position. A gesture of love from another is a crisis. What do we do? Who are we? Are we lovable persons who can accept the gesture of love? Are we unlovable persons who must—by virtue of who we think we are—reject that love?

A married man (let's call him Herb) became involved with another woman, and their involvement eventually led to her pregnancy. Herb's wife (let's call her Beth) was angry and hurt; but after counselling, offered her forgiveness and love to Herb once again. She wanted their marriage to continue; she wanted the relationship, which made Herb's act of infidelity possible, healed. Herb was thrust into a crisis situation. He could not believe that Beth would still love him and offer to continue their marriage. He had anticipated only rejection and divorce. He was so filled with guilt and remorse that he could not believe the offer of love. What was he to do? Could he embrace Beth's love and put behind himself his self-image which had led to his affair and was reinforced by it? Or would he be doomed to live with himself as he was? He was forced to judge himself in his decision—a decision to trust the love offered to him or to reject it. Herb had thought that Beth would be his judge. She would issue the verdict that he was beyond loving. But much to his surprise he found himself cast in the role of self-judge. This was his critical moment of decision.

Christ is God's offer of love to us, even amid our ceaseless unfaithfulness (see Hosea in the Old Testament). And that offer of love places us in a critical position of decision. It raises for us the question as to whether we are lovable, forgivable persons, or whether we are doomed to ourselves as we have been. The question which is forced on us is whether we can lay aside our old self-understanding to embrace a new self. So, paradoxically, we are forced to judge ourselves and determine our own destinies by responding either in belief or unbelief. Scandalously, God does not allow us to pass the responsibility of judgment on to him. He says dramatically in Christ (and most forcefully in the cross), "I love you," and thereby forces us to make our own decision and to pronounce our own judgment. John saw that one of the consequences of the fact of God's love for humans is that by that love humans are recast in the role of self-judges.

Having travelled the course of these three avenues we are brought finally to the destination toward which John so persistently directs us with his concepts of eternal life, resurrection, and judgment. That destination is the simple but profound idea that *now* is the moment of God's blessings. The richness of what God promises to the believer is not confined in the prison of the future but is free to inhabit the present moment of our existence. Heaven is on earth; heaven is now. Christians deprive themselves of the wealth of God's goodness to them when they rivet their eyes and minds on the future—on that blessing which awaits them beyond death. To do that is to suffer spiritual farsightedness. Our spiritual eyesight can discern the future blessings of God, but we are blind to the blessings in our present lives.

Too much of Christian thought is directed toward the future and too little toward the present. One of my ways of correcting this spiritual farsightedness among students has been to ask them this question: if Christianity did not offer the promise of life beyond the grave, would it still be a viable religious option? When they consider that question, many students find that their whole concept of Christianity is centered in what it offers in the way of life after death. They have reduced Christianity to a life-insurance policy against annihilation in death. And they are but typical of what comprises the thinking of far too many of us Christians. To be sure, Christianity does offer us a hope for survival of the grave, but it offers us so much more. It offers us a survival of the tombs of meaninglessness and a release from the graves of emptiness in the present. It offers us access to the depth of life's possibilities.

The scandal of Lent is that this Johannine Christ invites us to find bits and pieces of the heaven for which we so much yearn in the present moments of our lives. Amid our pain and suffering in this world, we live our heaven. Amid the afflictions of the personal tragedies each of us suffers, amid the agony of a distraught and broken world, there is resurrection, eternal life, and judgment. What an offense that is to our experience of anguish in this life! What a ridiculous proposition that is for those torn with conflict! And yet Christ would have us catch sight of and appropriate the richness of God's gift to us even amid that anguish.

One young pastor listening to the great theologian Karl Barth said of him: "He made me feel that tomorrow had already happened." John is telling us of the same experience which his Christian community had after listening to Christ. Christ makes the tomorrow of God's plan for his people happen today. Only our persistent farsightedness will prevent our experience of

God's tomorrows in our todays. But faith in the Christ corrects our spiritual vision. It allows us to continue to hold the future in view and still discern the present in all of its clarity. Can we allow Christ to correct our vision, or must the sufferings of the moment blind us to all but the future blessings of God?

Fifth Week:
The Scandal of Self-Hatred

John 12:25

For this chapter we focus on only one verse. But what a verse it is! Listen to this: "He who loves his life loses it, and he who hates his life in this world will keep it for eternal life."

This verse has been one of the most troublesome passages of the New Testament for me. The idea that I should be asked to hate myself is scandalous to me. My explication of this verse may be my own effort to rationalize my way out of part of the scandal of Lent. I am very conscious of the temptation to dilute these words, but I believe that is not what I have done. However, you should know that I am sensitive to that possibility and be alert to anything which you feel is less than an honest confrontation with the truth of these words.

THE CONTEXT AND OFFENSE OF 12:25

Our verse comes in the context of a pivotal passage in the gospel of John. Most scholars today regard Chapters 1 through 12 as constituting one-half of the gospel. They have been called, "the book of signs." They deal with the public ministry of Jesus. Chapters 13-21 have been labelled, "the book of glory," meaning that in these later chapters Jesus is, by Johannine terms, "glorified." They include first the private ministry of Jesus to his immediate circle of disciples and then the passion story itself. The latter half of Chapter 12 is the transition from the first phase of the ministry to the second. Jesus (or John) has spoken in the earlier chapters of the time when Jesus' "hour" will come (e.g., 2:4; 7:30; 8:20). Now John has Jesus say, "The hour *has come* for the Son of man to be glorified." This is the moment toward which the story has been building from the first. Jesus has entered Jerusalem; the death plot against him is fully planned. Jesus will go into seclusion with his disciples until the fateful time of his passion.

Tucked away in the midst of this transitional passage in 12:20-50 we encounter our verse. Jesus speaks of his impending death in a metaphor: the seed must die in the earth before it can spring forth and bear fruit (v. 24). Then the hard saying about loving or hating your life, followed by a challenge that those who believe in him must follow his path (v. 26).

The words of verse 25 have a familiar ring about them, for we find them in various forms elsewhere in the Gospels. (Compare them, for instance, with Mark 8:35; Luke 9:24 and 17:33; and Matt. 10:39.) We seem to be dealing with a reported saying of Jesus which was remembered and recorded in several different forms. John's version has impressed some scholars as the one which preserves most accurately the actual words of Jesus. Such a theory is based on two features of the Johannine version of the saying: First, the love-hate contrast is perhaps more likely in the original Aramaic language Jesus spoke than the contrast found in the other forms of the saying ("saves-loses," "seeks-loses," and "finds–loses"). Second, the saying is a perfect example of the kind of hyperbole or overstatement used by Jewish teachers at the time of Jesus. (See also Matt. 5:29-30.) We will want to consider below to what extent John 12:25 is exaggerated for teaching effect.

Now the offense of this message is really brought home. Maybe we can accept some of the scandalous ideas with which we have been presented thus far in John. Maybe we can buy the concept that Jesus would have to suffer and die. But now it is the disciple who must emulate the master. If Jesus' life is like a seed which must first die before it bears fruit (v. 24), the same is true for us. If this is not clear by implication, Jesus makes it clear in verse 26: "If any one serves me, he must follow me." It is no longer a matter of dealing with the scandal of offensive *ideas*. It is now a matter of dealing with the scandalous demands made on us. We are asked to hate our own lives and be able to accept the destiny of Jesus' earthly life as our own.

If there is anything we cherish, it is our own lives. Now we are asked to hate them! All of the human sciences—psychology, sociology, anthropology, etc.—seem to point in one clear direction. The human creature has a basic instinct for self-preservation. What is common to us and the animal world (among other things) is the concern to save our own lives. In one of his many interviews with children years ago, Art Linkletter asked a little boy what he wanted to be when he grew up. The little boy thought for a time and then said simply, "Alive!" Charles Schultz' creation, Snoopy, expressed the same point of view when he was trapped in his doghouse by a giant icicle. He dared not move for fear the heavy ice would come down, crushing him and his little house beneath its mighty weight. As Snoopy is contemplating his plight, he says, "I'm too *me* to die!" We all want to live. We all think that we are too "me" to die. Consequently, our basic drive is always and everywhere toward self-preservation.

But this verse offends the modern reader in a special way. Like many others, I have struggled (and continue to struggle) to love myself truly and properly. My problem has not been loving myself too much, but just the opposite. Like others, I have carried the burden of a self-concept which nurtured self-hatred and lack of self-esteem. The neurosis of many of us is that we have trouble accepting ourselves as we are. The result is that we are not able to love ourselves, much less others or even

God. Much therapy and many years of struggle are spent in helping people such as I learn to accept and love ourselves. Success finds us enabled to love ourselves and then able to love other people and our God. Moreover, the saving effect of the gospel is that the good news of God's love frees us to love ourselves. But now I am told that I must hate my life in this world. Just about the time I have begun to appreciate and accept myself, I encounter this enigmatic saying. I don't know about you, but I am offended—offended to the core!

How can we understand this terribly hard and scandalous saying? We are faced with a dilemma: we cannot simply neutralize the scandal of self-hatred. That would be to violate the basis of this entire book and would, more seriously, neutralize the heart of the Christian gospel. But on the other side of us lies an equally dangerous option. That is to take this saying at its face meaning and fit it into the distortion of our neurotic patterns of life. We have seen too much of that kind of thing: sick, neurotic people hating themselves under the guise of Christian devotion. So we are squeezed between two dangerous routes, both of which promise to lead us to a fraudulent Christianity. Is there a path between the two? I think there is a way of understanding this difficult passage which does not soften its demand on us but does preserve the necessity for positive self-esteem.

LOVING YOUR LIFE

The basic meaning of the verse is clear: if one loves his or her own life *above all else,* there is no chance to experience genuine life. This means, first of all, that anyone who embraces Christianity as a means to "save" themselves in the life beyond the grave has not captured the essence of the saying. This passage stands in judgment of those forms of Christian faith which stress above all else that we "save our souls" by believing. Christianity is not insurance for the next world—not insurance against extinction.

John Powell tells the story of the young man who was a confirmed atheist. He challenged Powell on more than one occasion in the college course Powell was teaching. Then the young man became seriously ill. The doctors told him there was nothing they could do and informed him he had only a short time to live. Then, amid his illness, the young man began frantically to search for God, pleading with God to make him well. After months of such efforts with no success, the young man finally despaired. He gave up his search for God. But soon after his resignation to his fate, he testified to Father Powell, there came to him a strange but certain sense of God's presence. So long as the young man sought God out of motives to save his own skin, he encountered only the muteness of God. But once his motives for finding God were cleared of such self-seeking, God made his presence known. Ours is not a faith that can authentically root in our own desire to better ourselves in any way.

But, secondly, the passage clearly affirms that there must be a love beyond our love of our own persons. Unless there is some transcending loyalty, life is never complete, never authentic. It is, in the words of John, not "eternal life." The Jewish psychiatrist, Viktor Frankl, relates in his book, *Man's Search for Meaning,* the centrality of some meaning beyond self. He was for a a time a prisoner in one of the Jewish concentration camps in Nazi Germany. The prisoners there, Frankl says, who had a meaning for life beyond themselves and their own survival somehow managed to endure the demeaning existence of prison life. For some it was the will to live and be united with their families; for others it was the solidity of their religious faith; and for Frankl it was his determination to live and reconstruct the book he had written just before his internment but which had been confiscated in his arrest. On the other hand, those who had no meaning which transcended their own selves seemed simply to give up and die. Without that overarching meaning, which pulled them beyond themselves into a higher realm of meaning, they lacked the will to persevere against the enormous difficulties of life in the concentration camp.

We are animals who are bent on self-preservation, but we are also creatures who need to live beyond ourselves. We are beings who must have a meaning which transcends ourselves.

What we have said about the meaning of the passage thus far does not negate but actually facilitates healthy self-acceptance and self-esteem. To say that I must have a greater love beyond myself does not deny that I must have a positive appreciation, acceptance, even love of myself. What the verse is addressing is the matter of *priorities*. If my self-love is my highest priority, genuine life is lost. But if that self-love stands in priority below a higher love, there is possibility for genuine life. This does not deny the importance of a healthy self-love but affirms the necessity of a higher love beyond one's self-love.

But we can claim even more. A love beyond one's self-love actually facilitates that self-love. To put it simply, we can feel good about ourselves only if we love something else more than we love ourselves. Perhaps part of the neurosis of America today is that we are so caught up in trying to love ourselves that there is nothing beyond ourselves. "Looking out for number one" has become the slogan of the American people. Authors and counselors who stress how to love yourself are making fortunes. But somehow the whole thing is not working. This obsession with self-love seems to be misdirected. Some interesting statistics appeared not long ago which compared the suicide rate among today's college-age adults with the rate among the same age group in the mid-1960s. The results of the comparison were revealing. The suicide rate today is markedly higher. There may be several explanations, but I submit that the young people of the mid-1960s were devoted to causes beyond themselves, such as social justice and the end of the war in southeast Asia. Whatever your evaluation of those young people and their efforts, you must admit that they had devotions which transcended themselves. In contrast, the college-age young people today for various and complex reasons generally lack those devotions. There is among them a clearly discernible concentration on themselves and their futures. They are preoccupied with insuring their economic futures and are noticeably passive regarding social and political issues. The fruits of such a concentration of attention are a frustration and meaninglessness which bar one from experiencing life as it should be and which understandably bring many to the utter despair of suicide.

When our loyalty lies beyond ourselves, genuine self-love is actually enhanced. Rather than diminishing self-love, a loyalty beyond self has the strange effect of making it possible to love ourselves. Perhaps you know the story of the little puppy who spent hours fruitlessly chasing its own tail. An old dog, having watched this behavior for some time, asked the puppy why he spent hours chasing his own tail. The puppy replied, "Because, sir, I find that happiness is in my tail, and I desire above all else to be happy." The wise old dog then said to the puppy, "I, too, find that happiness is in my tail, but I also find that as I go about my business my tail follows along naturally. I always have it, but it follows me. I don't have to chase it." Our verse suggests that self-love is lost or never attained when it is pursued for its own sake, but it follows naturally from our devotion to other loves beyond our self.

HATING YOUR LIFE

We have tried to articulate the possible meaning of this verse without yet facing squarely the difficulty of the second half of the saying: "The one who *hates* his or her own life in this world will preserve it for eternal life." We must now see if we can bring some light to bear more specifically upon those harsh words. The first thing to note is that our verse is fashioned in the form of ancient Hebraic parallelism. There are two lines, and the second line parallels the first, stating in a negative way what has been stated positively in the first line:

He who loves his life loses it,
And he who hates his life in this world will keep it for
eternal life.

When we see our passage as Hebrew poetry, we realize that the strong word, "hate," in the second line parallels in an opposite way the word, "love," in the first line. If then the meaning of the first line is, as I have argued, to love above all else, then the sense of "hate" in the second line is something like this: to regard as less important. The point is that we are dealing in these two strong words with the matter of preference (as Raymond E. Brown points out, *The Gospel According to John,* Vol. I, p. 467). To hate your life is to prefer it *below* something else. The matter of preference is expressed, however, in the strongest of terms. This is where it is helpful to understand that this verse is hyperbole. It is stated in its most stark, bold, and disturbing way. How weak it would have been if Jesus would have said, "Now if you prefer your own life, you will not be happy; but if you prefer the love of God, you will be happy." It loses its power. The attention it demands by its very exaggeration drives the listener to hear and wrestle with it. Nonetheless, when one has wrestled with it, you see that it is addressing the matter of preference and is not advocating self-hatred as such.

An explanation of the phrase, "in this world," may be helpful. "World" in the Fourth Gospel most often means not the physical world but the realm of evil, the realm of unbelief. "The world" used in a pejorative way in the gospel indicates those who are opposed to God. Rudolf Bultmann has contrasted the concepts of *world* and *creation* in order to elucidate the meaning of the former. *Creation* is living one's life in the recognition that all that is is derived from the Creator God. The *world,* on the other hand, is living one's life without that recognition and with the assumption that the universe and humans are independent of a Creator. The *world* is part of the massive dualism of the *gospel* in which the evangelist sets the life of unbelief over-against the life of faith. Persons of the *world* are persons who live as if God did not exist or is irrelevant. Hating our lives in this world means living not as persons of the world but living with a loyalty which is beyond ourselves and this realm.

"Eternal life" is then the opposite of "in this world." It is **a** quality of life rooted in God and his love. It is a life which is in tune with God's purpose for creation.

This exercise in interpretation suggests that the meaning of our verse might be paraphrased in this way: "One who loves only or above all else his or her own existence loses the authentic meaning of life. On the other hand, one who subjects his or her own self-love to a higher love discovers thereby life as it is intended by its Creator."

Our verse, then, does not teach self-hatred as such but actually implies that self-love is found (in the form of eternal life) when we subject it to a love which transcends self. But the crucial question is, have we thereby neutralized the verse and domesticated it so that the scandal of this hard saying has been eliminated? Not at all! Far from eliminating the offense of these words, I think that we have come face to face with it. And that offense is just this: we cannot genuinely love ourselves unless we love God and other persons more than we love ourselves. Self-love comes not from its own pursuit but from relegating it to a position of lesser importance.

This is not easy to swallow. It is especially difficult for a people such as ourselves who are inclined by instinct to look out above all for "big number one." It is difficult for those of us who are trapped in a culture which has discovered the importance of self-love for emotional health but has all of the wrong ideas about how to attain it. The offense is that we are asked by Jesus to give up our frantic quest to become lovable people to ourselves. That shakes us to the core. And it is not as if we can say, "Okay, we will give it a try." Then we go about pretending to love other people and God, but each evening we pull out the dipstick of our emotions to see if our self-love has increased a bit. Such an effort makes a mockery of loving others above ourselves and is aimed ultimately not at being other-directed but is simply another perverse form of selfishness. The point is we do not love others *in order that we may love ourselves.* The old dog does not keep looking back to check and make sure his tail is coming along with him. He forgets his tail, and then, sure enough, it follows him everywhere.

No, we go this way with Jesus completely or not at all. We decide once and for all that other people and their well-being and God are absolutely, unequivocally more important than ourselves. If we do, there follows a self-esteem which all the efforts to seek self-love can never know. This is consistent with the general theme of the teaching of Jesus. Rudolf Bultmann observed that Jesus spoke of rewards for righteousness, but "he promises reward to those who are obedient without thought of reward" (*Jesus and the Word*, p. 79). There is the reward of self-love for those who will put God's love above self-love, but that reward is for precisely those who love God and others without thought of the reward.

In elementary physics one learns that when an object moves rapidly around a center there are two resulting forces. The one is a centripetal force which tends to pull the object toward the center of the orbit. There is also a centrifugal force which tends to pull the object away from the center of the orbit. There are comparable forces in the orbits of our personalities. On the one hand, there is a selfish force which tends to pull us into ourselves. It tugs at us, constantly nudging us into the quest for self-love on its own. But there is also an equally strong force inviting us outward. It pulls us away from ourselves and into the lives of other people and ultimately into God's life. It beckons us to reach beyond ourselves for our highest love. It is that second force—the centrifugal force of our personalities— which is the pull of the Holy Spirit. But we can yield to either force. It is our choice. We can seek first of all our own self-love, or we can seek above all else to love God through loving other people. The scandalous proclamation of the gospel is that if we seek the first we lose precisely what it is we are seeking; but if we seek the second we gain the first as well. Can we believe that? No, that is not the question. The question is, can we *practice* that? Can we commit ourselves to a life of loving others above our own selves and thereby find what we cannot find by searching for it, namely, our self-love?

Maundy Thursday:
The Scandal of Servanthood

John 13:1-17

On the solemn evening of what has come to be called Maundy Thursday, we customarily gather to recall and recreate the last supper Jesus shared with his disciples before his death. Quite properly, we celebrate the sacrament of Holy Communion on the occasion of what the New Testament tells us was Jesus' institution of that meal. The gospels of Matthew, Mark, and Luke, along with Paul (1 Cor. 11:23-26), all witness to the fact that the Eucharist takes its roots in that last supper. Christians cannot allow this occasion to pass without participation in the sacrament.

Yet the gospel of John surprises us with its silence about the institution of the sacrament of the Eucharist. John tells us about the evening before Jesus' death and about the last supper he shared with the disciples. But John has no account of the Eucharistic act of Jesus. No feature of the gospel of John has caused such consternation and such debate as has the fact that the Eucharist is nowhere mentioned. How could the evangelist have ignored such a crucial event for the Christian community?

JOHN'S "MAUNDY THURSDAY"

There are various ways of understanding the absence of the institution of the Eucharist from John's narrative—some of them reasonable and some of them mere reflections of what some would like to think was the case. However, John's silence about the sacraments should be the occasion for probing this gospel more deeply. Perhaps we should spend our time and energies not so much in trying to understand why John omitted the institution of the Eucharist but in attempting to understand what John says in place of that event.

We begin reading the account of the Last Supper in John's gospel, and we ready ourselves for those old familiar words— "Jesus took bread," etc.—but there is a shock in store for us. John narrates the story of the meal, even including a reference to the evil plan of Judas. But then when the scene is set for the first enactment of the Eucharistic meal, John startles us with another narrative: Jesus washes the feet of his disciples. Now we do not want to pretend to know that John intended this story as some sort of substitute for the account of the institution of the Eucharist. But he clearly believed that this story of the footwashing was appropriate for (what we call) a Maundy Thursday setting; it was a fitting consideration for the evening of the day before Jesus' death. As scandalous as it is to embrace a gospel that does not tell us about the institution of the Lord's Supper, perhaps we had better listen with care to what it has to say about that memorable occasion.

Notice in John's narrative that the act of foot washing follows immediately upon the statement that Jesus knew what Judas had in mind (v. 3). His act of washing the feet of the disciples stands in the context of his consciousness of that fate awaiting him later that evening and the next day. This observation of John's setting for the footwashing is worth our attention later on.

The narrative now proceeds to the act of the washing itself, broken by the conversation with Peter (vv. 6-11). Peter's resistance to Jesus offers the occasion for the first of the comments by Jesus as to the meaning of his strange act. After that, with the greatest economy, John completes the narrative in verse 12. There follows the beginning of Jesus' discourse. He first offers still additional words regarding the meaning of his act (vv. 12b-17). Then Jesus slips into a long, long discourse, broken with some narrative and dialog only in 13:22-30; 13:36-38; and 14:8-9. The long discourse, commonly called the farewell discourse, begins after the account of the washing of the disciples' feet. This long speech by Jesus in which he contemplates the meaning of his ministry, his forthcoming death, and the future of the disciples is the building for which the footwashing narrative constitutes the front porch.

We shall not labor over any of the other details in the account but get on to the focus of our chapter. Peter expresses what for many of us is our reaction to this remarkable act of Jesus: "Lord, do you wash my feet? . . . You shall never wash my feet!" (vv. 6, 8). Peter is scandalized by the behavior of his master. This one whom Peter has come at long last to understand as God's special agent to rescue his people cannot do such a demeaning task! What is the Son of God doing on his knees bathing the dirty, sweaty, smelly feet of this motley band of followers? Let me ask you: what would your reaction be should the Christ appear to you dressed in the garb of a servant, armed with a basin of water, and about to bathe your feet? With Peter we would shout in protest, "No, no, Lord, you can't do this! This is not befitting your office." How scandalous that the Christ should undertake such a deed. "Behave yourself, Lord. Act like the Lord and God that you are. You are embarassing us all!"

It is offensive to our regard for him. It is offensive to the world that one who professes to be who he is should behave like this. What possible meaning could such an act have?

We must cut into the scandal of the footwashing by asking how John himself understood this bewildering act. Our incision into the narrative reveals two different accounts of the meaning that can be assigned to this act. Jesus speaks first to Peter about

78

its meaning in verses 7-8 and then again to the whole body of his disciples in 12b-17. The scandal of the footwashing is explained—or perhaps only intensified—in two distinct but related ways in these two passages.

CLEANSED BY LOVE

In response to the protest of Peter, Jesus is made to say, "What I am doing you do not know now, but afterward you will understand. . . . If I do not wash you, you have no part in me" (vv. 7-8). What do these words mean? They and everything about this narrative point us to one unavoidable conclusion about the meaning of the footwashing: We are witnessing a symbolic portrayal of the meaning of the forthcoming crucifixion.

Consider, first, the fact that John introduces his account of the passion story with this narrative of the footwashing. Like a table of contents, it points our way through the subsequent events to their climax. It is like a road map telling us where the route of the passion story will lead. Consider, too, the fact which we have already pointed out, namely, that Jesus undertakes this act of footwashing in the context of a knowledge of Judas' plans. John wants us to understand, I think, that Jesus acts in this way to inform his disciples of the meaning of the tragic course of the next 24 hours. The footwashing is like a dying man telling his loved ones what he regards to be the meaning of his life and approaching death.

John frames the narrative in such a way, then, to make his readers aware that this is a prophetic act symbolizing the meaning of the crucifixion. How appropriate that Jesus should communicate the meaning of his forthcoming death with the symbolism of an act.

And actions do speak louder than words, as we are frequently told. We know that to be true. I can utter the words, "I love you," in every variation conceivable; but my acts of love will say far more than all those words. That anonymous lover who long ago declared, "I'd climb the highest mountain or swim the deepest ocean for you," knew that acts of love are more powerful than words of love. Often the gestures of love are the most effective means of communication—the embrace, the kiss, the warm touch. It is in the context of this truth that the Old Testament prophets so often chose to summarize their message to the people of Israel through powerful and symbolic acts. Remember Isaiah's strange act? He went naked and barefoot for three years as a sign and warning that the Assyrians would strip naked and take into exile those who tried to rebel against them (Isa. 20). Remember, too, Jeremiah's equally strange act? He wore over his shoulders an oxen yoke to symbolize God's intention to put Judah under the yoke of the rule of Babylonia (Jeremiah 27). Jesus' washing the feet of his disciples is in that great tradition of using a powerful act to communicate a profound message.

But what does John understand this powerful and symbolic act to communicate? This vivid manifestation of Jesus' love of his disciples means that his forthcoming suffering and death are manifestations of the love of God. What more loving thing could Jesus have done on that last night than to have washed the feet of his followers? And that gesture of love foreshadows the supreme gesture of love—his obedient death on the cross. Like a sneak preview of the coming attraction, the footwashing anticipates and summarizes the crucial act by which God expresses his love of humanity through the death of his Son. That is why Jesus says to Peter, "afterward [after the climax of the passion] you will understand" (v. 7). What Jesus here expresses in this graphic action, he elsewhere articulates verbally: "Greater love has no man than this, that a man lay down his life for his friends" (15:13). "Unless a grain of wheat falls into the earth and dies, it remains alone; but if it dies, it bears much fruit" (12:24). Or in the words of the evangelist, "For God so loved the world that he gave his only Son" (3:16).

It is, however, not only the manifestation of God's love in the cross toward which the footwashing points. It points as well toward the effect of that love in the lives of all who comprehend it. Jesus replies to Peter's protests, "If I do not wash you, you have no part in me" (v. 10), and then goes on to speak about washing and cleansing. The love expressed in the cross, like the love enacted in the footwashing, has the effect of cleansing. The meaning of the footwashing is that the love of God, to be manifested in the suffering and death of Jesus, bathes the believer and makes him or her clean.

At the foundation of this narrative is the simple fact that love has a cleansing effect in human personality. The love of one person for another washes away the grime of impurities. Think of the impurities you have seen washed down the drain by love: the demobilizing sense of insecurity; the loneliness of feeling as if one does not belong anywhere; the hoplessness of having no meaning for life; the subtle tendency toward self-destruction; and, most important, the fatality of believing that one is unlovable.

You have heard it said so many times and have witnessed it in your own family or acquaintances: a young adult is wasting away her or his life in behavior which eventually is destructive. Then that young person meets another, love blossoms, and they marry. We say, in popular parlance, "He or she really settled down." What we mean, I think, is that the love of the other rinsed out those feelings and attitudes which motivated such senseless behavior. Every counselor knows the power of love to bathe a human personality. Every parent knows the power of love to wash away the impurities which can clog the spirit of a child. Every spouse knows the power of love to scrub away the dirt that stains one's life.

The footwashing symbolizes the cleansing power of love in its most potent form. The love of God expressed in the cross cleans out the human life as washing the feet cleans off the dust of a day's travel. What a powerful symbol this footwashing is. In a simple act it captures the meaning which Christians struggle to express. It articulates through human behavior the depths of meaning in God's act in Christ which human language only feebly represents.

But there is a scandal here! Not just the scandal of the Son of God engaging in such a demeaning act — that is scandal enough! But the scandal of allowing another's love to cleanse us. That, too, is an offensive possibility to us humans. To accept the gesture of love from another as the act which straightens our bent and deformed lives is to accept a degree of dependence which makes us uncomfortable. Do you sometimes feel, as I do, a strange reluctance to allow another person to do something loving for you? Another wants to give me an unexpected and free gift out of her love for me. I resist. "Oh, you don't have to do that," I protest. Why a reluctance to be loved? Because love breeds dependence, and we don't like to be dependent, do we? But powerful love also carries with it an invitation to commitment. To receive love from another is to be called on to make a loving commitment in response. We are offended by love, because we fear the commitment which the acceptance of that love will evoke from us.

God's cleansing love in Christ offends us because it is an invitation to love in return and to commit ourselves to a relationship of love. Such a commitment brings obligation and responsibility: it sucks us out of our inner-directed worlds and pulls us into other-directedness. It offends our comfortable world of ego-centeredness and turns us inside out. It is a scandal that God should love us with such a cleansing love, not because we would not like to be clean, but because of the cost to ourselves imposed by that love.

INVITED TO SERVANTHOOD

Our incision into the footwashing has brought us to the heart of the scandal of this act—but not quite. The sense in which the footwashing is a symbolic portrayal of the meaning of the cross is expressed in the dialog between Peter and Jesus. But there is another related meaning expressed in the words of Jesus upon the completion of the washing. In verses 12-17 Jesus speaks of the meaning of what he has just done: "Do you know what I have done to you?" And the point is simple: "I have given

you an example, that you also should do as I have done to you."
To receive this cleansing love evokes a commitment to a comparable love. The love of God in Christ calls forth the love of humans for one another. As Jesus has done, we are invited to do to one another. As the scholars say, the ethical injunction arises out of the theological premise.

In some Christian traditions the words of Jesus are taken literally and understood as the near equivalent (or even, in some cases, as the equivalent) of the institution of a sacrament. In those traditions, footwashing is practiced as a faithful obedience to the words of Jesus, "You should do as I have done to you." Not a bad idea, when you think about it: washing the feet of other Christians of your community as a sign of your love. But the words of Jesus have, of course, a broader application. It is not his act of washing the feet of his disciples alone which is to be imitated; it is his servant posture which we are to assume. If Jesus, who is Lord and Teacher, can assume the posture of a servant toward his disciples, we all can be servants of one another in every way.

This theme is typical of John's understanding of Christian life. The imperatives for Christian behavior (and there are few of them expressed in the gospel of John) are rooted in the relation of Jesus to his disciples and to his Father. Christians are to love others as the Father has loved the Son and as the Son has loved the disciples (17:23 and 15:12). Christians are to be one, as the Father and Son are one (17:11). Christians have a mission, as the Father sent the Son into the world on a mission (17:18). The example of Christian behavior is seen in the relationship of Christ with God and with his disciples.

Here then we stand in the presence of the scandal of servanthood. It is a two-edged sword, this scandal: the Lord God himself in the form of his Son on earth is none other than the servant of the people; and Christians are then to take up that servanthood as their own style of life, imitating the example of their Lord. Our minds are offended: the Lord God ought not to behave like a servant. Our spirits are offended: we ought not to have to behave like servants. This simple story of the footwashing finally scandalizes both our theology and our pride. How dare he act so "ungodlike" by being a servant to his subjects! How dare he ask us to become servants like him! (One is reminded of Paul's admonition to humility, which is also based on a view of Christ in Phil. 2:5-8). We follow one who came among us as a servant and coaxes us to become servants.

There once lived an executive of a large firm who behaved in a very unorthodox and unexecutive manner. It was his practice to arrive each morning long before others in the building which housed the central offices of his corporation. He would then spend the first hour of his work day going from one office to another preparing coffee. In each office he would begin the coffee brewing in preparation for the arrival of his staff (a menial task too often assigned to female secretaries). When the workers arrived, they found fresh warm coffee awaiting them— from the least of them (the lowly errand boys) to the most important (the powerful executives). At first the workers were puzzled by the mysterious presence of the coffee, but gradually the word leaked out as to who was responsible. The reactions were varied. Some were deeply impressed by the fact that "the big boss" would undertake such a lowly task. The effect of their leader's behavior was to make them more dedicated workers and to evoke from them an attitude of helpfulness toward their colleagues. Others, however, found their chief's behavior inappropriate. They questioned his motives: "He's trying to get something from us." They questioned his sanity: "The old boy has slipped over the edge." They were offended by the idea that they were, by implication, supposed to treat their subordinates in a comparable manner. Such unseemly behavior on the part of the executive even caused some to look for employment elsewhere, fearful as they were of the implications of his behavior for their jobs. Many felt not only uncomfortable but downright offended by the violation of the structure of authority and responsibility occasioned by their highest superior. Among those, however, who responded favorably to his actions, there emerged a sense of community and congeniality unparalled in the business world.

Our Chief Executive has acted in a very unexecutive manner. Behaving like a slave of his subjects rather than as their master, he has washed the feet of his followers. That humble servanthood repels some. It disgusts their sense of propriety. It perturbs their perception of convention. But that humble servanthood moves others to similar behavior. Among them there arises a sense of a community of servants. They care for one another; their style of life together is marked by an ethos of mutual support. They are almost like a human body, each part in its own way functioning to serve the total organism.

The scandal of servanthood is central to the scandal of Lent. It is the lifeblood flowing through the course of those ocurrences which comprise the body of the Lenten story. Still, it is that feature of Lent which evades our understanding and our response. The scandal of servanthood is the offense which we would like most to neutralize, to defuse. We neither understand how our God—Lord, Creator, and Sustainer of this vast universe—could become a servant to us humans; nor do we believe that we have it in us to cut our lives along the pattern of that example of servanthood. The little girl, frightened by the suspenseful story on the television, closed her eyes to hide herself from what might be about to happen. We close our eyes as we approach the climax of this Lenten drama in which we have been participating for the past five weeks. We close our eyes because we want to hide ourselves from what might be about to happen to us. As scandalous as it is, the cloak of divine servanthood might be dropped down over us. Try as we can, we might just be pulled down from the tower of rank and status we have constructed for ourselves and be found among the caste of servants.

John seems an intruder into our Maundy Thursday celebration. And he brings with him an ominous voice. It is the voice of the servant, Jesus, whose body and blood were given as a final and unequivocal statement of God's serving love for us. We eat the bread and drink the wine which are the body and blood of a

Lord who was a servant. As surely as we ingest these into our bodies, we will be infected with that servant impulse which motivated his death. Beware, lest this sacrament of bread and wine make a servant of you, even as they are the signs of Christ's servanthood. The scandal of servanthood you see resides in this Eucharistic meal. And its scandalous effects may well make a different person of you—a clean person, a servant person.

Good Friday:
The Scandal of Crucifixion

John 3:13-15

Imagine, if you can, this scenario: a small religious group in America catches the headlines with their novel beliefs. They claim that their leader was divine. But that same leader has just been convicted of a crime, sentenced to be put to death, and executed in the electric chair. The leader's ignoble death, however, has not deterred the faithful followers. On the contrary, they now claim that his disgraceful death was still a further reflection of his divine nature. Our reactions to such a group would doubtless be disdain. "How weird," we might think to ourselves. "These days you can find somebody to believe most anything."

And yet, of course, our imaginary scenario is comparable to the situation of the early Christians. Their master—this one they believed to be the Messiah of Israel—had suffered the most disgraceful kind of death known. It bore implications, labeling Jesus a socially undesirable person. It was the kind of death preserved for those who had been found to be dangerous to the social fabric and the political order. It is no wonder, then, that the majority of those in the Roman Empire of the first century laughed at the claims being made by Christians for this Jesus (1 Cor. 1:23).

THE SCANDAL OF CRUCIFIXION

The central scandal of Christianity has always been the crucifixion. Even the claim that Christ survived death and appeared to his followers could not neutralize the offensiveness of the fact of his death. To that central scandal the entire New Testament witnesses boldly and honestly. It was the task of the early Christian preachers to convince the skeptical listeners that Jesus' death was not what it appeared to be. And you can imagine that sort of a task! It was a selling job that would challenge the most skillful salesperson. The earliest Christians were asking their listeners to believe what must have sounded like outrageous and incredible claims. Those listeners thought they knew how God would act and what his agent on earth would be like and do. The earliest Christians had first to convince them that their notions were erroneous. That would be like trying to sell a goodluck charm to a group of experimental psychologists. It is, I suppose, an indication of the truth of Christianity that it survived and grew in spite of the burden of proclaiming a central figure whose death represented such a defamation. The hinge upon which Christianity turns is one which appears to most humans as decisive proof of the error of this religious movement.

The New Testament contains a number of different interpretations of the meaning of the death of Jesus, all intended among other things to demonstrate that its deeper meaning contradicts its scandalous appearance. One interpretation which is found in several parts of the New Testament is the claim that Jesus' death was a redemptive sacrifice (e.g., Rom. 3:25). This interpretation of the death of Jesus took a central place in Christian thought until today it is one of the basic affirmations of our faith.

But one of the mind-expanding things about the gospel of John is the fact that this evangelist and his church seem to have a somewhat different interpretation of the death of Jesus. To read John honestly and openly is like being introduced to a whole new dimension of Christian thought about the death of Jesus. Some of you are old enough to remember the first time you ever heard stereophonic music. For those of us raised on monophonic, stereo music seemed to be a totally new world of sound. The basic theme was still there just as we heard it on monophonic, but now there was a new dimension. This additional dimension added a fullness to the music that made us realize how much we had missed.

The analogy works well for the Johannine view of the death of Jesus. It is not that the gospel denies the redemptive dimension of the meaning of the death of Christ. But the redemptive meaning of the death of Jesus is almost a minor theme in the gospel as compared with the one we are about to discuss. What the gospel of John seems to be saying to us is that the meaning of the death of Jesus cannot be reduced to one point.

Let me draw out still another analogy. Abstract painting is intended to be rich enough in meaning to say several things at the same time. You cannot reduce good modern abstract art to one simple meaning. It is loaded with meanings, so that it must be studied and discussed by many people over a period of time before its meaning is fully understood. John knew that the death of Jesus was loaded with meaning. It could not be captured in one point—the sacrificial redemption of humanity. And it seems to have been John's intent to show us another meaning inherent in the crucifixion.

But it was also his intent to face squarely the scandalous character of that death and to claim that the scandal is at the heart of the Christian gospel. To say that the death of Jesus is a sacrifice which atones for human sin is also to claim that the scandalous death is not what it appears to be; but for John *the scandal is the gospel*. In an even more direct way than Paul (or other parts of the New Testament) John invites us to find in the very offensiveness of the cross its attractiveness.

CRUCIFIXION AS "LIFTING UP"

Our passage for consideration in this chapter is an enigmatic and elusive one which presents us with a nutshell version of the Johannine understanding of the death of Christ. It comes at the end of the conversation with Nicodemus in John 3. John first articulates an important understanding of the identity of Christ in verse 13. Christ is the one who has descended from his heavenly home and will once again ascend there. Much of the Johannine view of Christ is woven out of such a descent-ascent model of thinking about Christ. But our major concern is not with that point but what follows it. In verse 14 he has Jesus make this puzzling allusion to the Old Testament story found in Num. 21:6ff. There we are told how the people of Israel, wandering in the desert, are plagued with serpents whose bites are fatal to the people. The serpents, we are told, are God's punishment for the sinfulness of the people. They realize their sin and go to Moses in repentance. Moses then prays for the people, and God instructs him as to how to relieve this punishment. Moses fashions a serpent of bronze, places it on a stake, and lifts it up over the people. Those who look at the bronze serpent lifted above them are healed of the bites of the poisonous serpents. John says, "as Moses lifted up the serpent in the wilderness, so must the Son of Man be lifted up, that whoever believes in him may have eternal life" (v. 15).

The use of the Old Testament allusion seems strange to our ears, but the point appears to be this: as the elevated serpent brought health to the Hebrews, so Christ's elevation brings healing (salvation or, in Johannine terms, eternal life) to humanity. John Wesley wrote of this verse, "All those who look to Him by faith recover spiritual health, even as all that looked at that serpent recovered bodily health" (*Explanatory Notes on the New Testament,* p. 313). This is what the scholars call a typological interpretation of the Old Testament, meaning that in the Old Testament one finds a pattern of action which in Christ is repeated and fulfilled. But the main point of our attention is the parallel between the lifting up of the serpent and the lifting up of Christ.

John uses this word, "lifted up," frequently as a way of referring to the crucifixion. (A few other examples are 8:28; 12:32; and 12:34). It is unique to John that this word should be used to refer to the crucifixion; nowhere else in the New Testament do we have it used in quite the way John uses it. Actually, it is an ambiguous word in Greek. It could be used to describe the process of lifting a person onto a cross for execution; but it could also be used for the process of enthroning a king—lifting the person onto the throne and up to the status of monarch. Hence, the single word had two rather different meanings, depending on the context in which it was used. We find the same sort of thing in our language. Take, for instance, the word, "bridge." Used in one context, it refers to a structure which spans a river or a chasm. Used in another context, it refers to an instrument used to measure electrical impedance.

What John is telling us in using the ambiguous word, "lifted up," to refer to the crucifixion is startling. He is suggesting that the act which is the ignominious means of death is also in the case of Jesus the act which is the exaltation of the world's king. Ironically, in putting Jesus to death, his executioners have enthroned him! What was intended to be the disgracing of this prophet from Galilee was in fact his coronation. John makes the same point when he reports that the inscription placed on the cross read in Hebrew, Latin, and Greek, "Jesus of Nazareth, the King of the Jews" (19:19-20). Although he intended derision, Pilate unknowingly proclaimed Christ's coronation to the world in its three languages. John not only loves to use words which are significantly laden with more than one meaning; he loves to narrate actions which have double meanings—the practice of telling an event which has one meaning on the surface but still another below the surface.

But John also tells us about his unique view of the death of Jesus when he has Jesus speak of his impending glorification. After Jesus concludes his public ministry and begins his extended discussions in private with his disciples, he speaks repeatedly of his impending glorification. Most impressive perhaps is the statement at 13:31. Judas Iscariot has just left the circle of the disciples to begin his act of betrayal. "When he [Judas] had gone out, Jesus said, 'Now is the Son of man glorified.'" John frequently has Jesus speak of the approaching death as a *glorification*. What this tells us is once again that the crucifixion in the Fourth Gospel is conceived ironically as the enthronement of Jesus.

But we are in touch here with an even more profound Johannine view. To put it as simply as possible, it is that John has compressed what for others was two (or even three) separate acts into one. The crucifixion for John is the exaltation of Jesus. John does not really insist that the crucifixion needs the resurrection as a kind of reversal of humiliation into glorification. In much of the New Testament it is this way: the crucifixion is the humiliation of Christ; the resurrection is the glorification. (Luke adds still a third: the ascension of Christ.) But in the gospel of John Jesus is never really humiliated. His crucifixion is never a bringing down of this man. The Johannine Jesus deports himself like a king throughout his trial and execution. It is significant that John (along with Luke) does not report the word of Jesus from the cross which most vividly depicts his humiliation, "My God, my God, why have you forsaken me?" (Matt. 27:46 and Mark 15:34). Jesus for John is never broken, never separated from God, and never disgraced. His glory, which he carried from the first, is carried through the experience even of his passion.

What then is the function of the resurrection for John? It seems to be the *revelation of his glory* to his disciples. It is not the glorification itself, as it seems to have been for Matthew and Luke and even Paul; but it is simply the informing of the disciples of that glory.

Can we make this point more clear? Paul would seem to think that Jesus was like a king who cast aside all of his royal prerogatives to live among his people for a time (Phil. 2:6-11). In the course of his sojourn among his people he suffers mortification at their hands; but then (in the resurrection) he is restored to his royal throne and dignity. John would tell the story more like this: Jesus never put aside his royal prerogatives; he never shed the glory of his office. He moved among the people as their king. Some, however, think that he is a false king. They try as best they can to break the "pretender" and reveal his true identity. They even try to put him to death as a means of forcing him to shed his disguise. But their efforts are of no avail, for Christ is truly their king. He endures the worst they can do to him without ever losing his royal dignity or composure. He actually moves above and beyond all of this. Then, for those who had not yet "beheld his glory" in its fullness—a glory which had never been dimmed through all of this—he made it abundantly clear in the resurrection appearances. The king has always been the king and still is the king! Consequently, John has no need for a resurrection which reenthrones the glorious king.

John has faced the scandal of the cross in a new way. He has turned that scandal into a positive thing, not by portraying it as a sacrificial death, but as the enthronement and demonstration of Jesus' kingship, which had never been compromised by his passion. But, on the other hand, John has put the scandal of the cross in even more brutal terms. The death of the Messiah is his exaltation! If that imaginary religious group we mentioned at the first of this chapter were to claim that the death of their leader was a heroic action which freed them in some way, we might be able to understand their strange claims. But if they were to say that the electric chair was the coronation of the king of the world, we would flinch even more.

THE ENTHRONEMENT OF DIVINE LOVE

Here is the scandal of Lent in its severest form: the enthronement of the Messiah King is a crucifixion. Where we would expect pomp and circumstance and universal recognition, we get instead the dismal, degrading death of this Messiah figure—a death as a common criminal. Yet John says that this is the decisive act which glorifies Christ. What can we say? Is John not suggesting at this point divine and human values are so far apart that we humans cannot even recognize the divine? Is he not saying that God's values lie precisely in one who will suffer and die? The king is one who will lay down his life for his friends (15:13). I suggest that the key to the way in which John could understand the cross as an exaltation is found in a verse which stands just ahead of our passage—John 3:16. God loved the world of humans so much that he gave his Son, and the crucifixion is the manifestation of that love for all to see. The scandal of the cross is that God's love is a misfit in this world of ours. It is a square peg that doesn't fit in a round hole.

A love that goes so far as a cross is a love which is divine. There may be a modern version of this gospel of ours disguised in a recent motion picture, *The Deer Hunter* (screenplay by Deric Washburn). There is an obvious love and affection among this group of men who are prisoners of the Viet Cong. And one of them, Nick, can never free himself of the horror of being forced by his captors to play "Russian roulette." In a strange and obsessive way, after his release he remains in Saigon playing the deadly game for the entertainment of a deranged group of gamblers. Michael's love for Nick finally brings him back to Saigon in search for his friend. Having found him, he tries in vain to bring him out of his psychotic stupor. Finally, Michael goes to the gambling table to play the insane game with Nick as a way of trying to bring his friend back to sanity. That supreme gesture of love—his willingness to put a bullet through his own head if it will awaken Nick—by human standards is foolhardy and fruitless. But it enthrones human love in the film as nothing else could do.

For the eyes of faith, John is saying, there is in the crucifixion, the revelation of the love of God which brings humans out of their stupor of alienation and into the realm of genuine life. Yet only the power of faith can penetrate the enigmatic mystery of the cross. Michael's gesture of love was foolish to the human mind, yet, for those willing to see, it manifested the power of love. Christ's death on the cross was a scandal to the human mind, yet, for those willing to see, it manifested the power of divine love. The cross is no humiliation precisely because it is the supreme act of divine love. Only the distorted vision of the world of unbelief could fail to see that love.

Years ago an eye infection forced me to have one eye bandaged. For about a week I lived and worked with only one functioning eye. The result was that I learned firsthand the fact that it is the two eyes working together which provides the human with much of the sense of depth perception. I found that with only one eye I could not judge the distance between my hand, for instance, and my cup of coffee. I was constantly overestimating or underestimating distances.

I suggest that John is saying that if you look at the cross with one eye you see only the dimension of disgrace. But if you add the eye of faith you see the other dimension. With faith you can see there the love of God enacted in its pure form. With but one eye, the cross is an offense; with two eyes and the power of faith perception, it is the exaltation of love. The double meaning of the word, "lifted up," is John's way of suggesting that we must see the faith dimension of the cross, or else we see only a miserable death!

Perhaps the reason John and his community chose to understand the death of Jesus the way they did is found precisely here in what we have been saying about the cross as a declaration of love. The king of love is not humiliated in his death. On the contrary, his death is the enthronment of all that he stands for. It is the elevation of love to its proper place. Love is not disgraced in one who gives up his or her life for their friends. It is honored, glorified, and crowned.

A friend heard that a pastor had taken time out of his busy schedule to help a lonely, destitute, and friendless man move his belongings to a new apartment in the city. The friend challenged the pastor's wisdom in using his time in this way and finally asked, "Isn't it demeaning of a person of your status to put on work clothes and carry boxes?" The pastor replied, "No, I think it is loving." Love is not disgraced by the lowest of services; it is fulfilled. Love was not scandalized in the death of Jesus; it was epitomized.

Before us stands the issue. Can we dare to embrace a love which does not feel scandal or disgrace but goes to the extreme to find its true expression? Can we dare to see in the scandalous death of Jesus the expression of what love is all about? The cross of love does scandalize our human sense of love. It offends that love which in the comfort of affluence and status is satisfied with acts which never inconvenience. It punctures such a pseudo-love with painful jabs. It makes us ask if we have not acculturated our understanding of Christian love. We have made a piece of jewelry out of the cross. We fashion crosses of beautiful and precious metals and adorn our churches, our homes, and our bodies with them. Have we also made the love of the cross into an innocuous and culturally acceptable ideal?

The scandal of the cross is that it forces us to examine our understanding of the love of God and the love which God asks of us. To face that scandal squarely is to ask if we can live and teach a love that does not know humiliation in a death that is for others.

Easter:
The Scandal of Doubt

John 20:24-29

We have come to the surprising conclusion of our Lenten journey. The journey appeared to have ended with those words of Jesus spoken from the cross with such finality: "It is finished" (19:30). Yet there is another scene. There is the recounting of that first Easter morning and the subsequent Easter experiences of the first Christians. The plot has been dramatically turned.

Easter is a scandal. On that point the entire New Testament agrees. That this crucified criminal, Jesus of Nazareth, should arise from his tomb and appear to his disciples is a claim of incredible proportions. It is that fact which constitutes the trunk of the scandal of Easter. But there are additional limbs of that trunk of scandal, and it is in the gospel of John alone that we find one of those scandalous limbs. It is, of course, the story of the doubt of Thomas. That account of a resurrection appearance is set within John's unique retelling of the first Easter. He first narrates the discovery of the empty tomb by Mary Magdalene, who in turn brings Simon Peter and "the beloved disciple" to see for themselves (20:1-10). The first appearance of the resurrected Christ is to Mary, as she remains outside the empty tomb, weeping over the fearful meaning of this discovery she has made (20:11-18). "On the evening of that day," John tells us, Christ appeared to the disciples behind doors locked in fear (20:19-23). But Thomas was not among them at that time; John then recounts the second appearance of the resurrected Christ to the disciples—this time with Thomas among them (20:24-29). With that narrative John seems to have felt his gospel properly concluded, and he appends his closing remark (20:30-31). (It is quite apparent that Chapter 21 is either a later addition to the gospel or else a misplaced fragment of narrative which originally belonged earlier in the document.)

John's account of the appearance to Thomas is more than another resurrection story; it is the climactic conclusion of this entire gospel. Into this story, John packs the ultimate meaning of his entire narrative. In so many fine novels, the last few pages reveal the meaning which the novelist has intended his or her story to convey. There the powerful insights and the succinct summaries of meaning are articulated. So, with John's narrative, this last episode illumines the previous pages from the prologue to the resurrection stories.

THOMAS' DOUBT

It is then important that John should present us in this final episode with the scandal of doubt. It is provocative that he should structure this last dramatic and summarizing scene around the experience of unbelief and show the path from doubt to what John surely wants us to understand to be genuine and mature faith.

But how odd that he should make doubt the central theme of this last scene! To our minds, doubt is sin. Doubt is the opposite of faith. It is destructive of faith and makes war on all that we struggle to hold as true. We are offended by the possibility that Thomas' doubt should be the occasion for the birth of what John regards as the most authentic faith found in his narrative. We pity the doubter and wish for the doubter an escape from the bonds of disbelief. But never do we want to entertain the possibility that doubt might be the catalyst for genuine faith.

Yet there is something about this Thomas figure that is strangely appealing to us. He expresses a common, human demand—the demand for concrete experience on which to base religious faith. He wanted to see for himself the risen Lord. He would not be content with secondhand knowledge. He would not believe that Jesus had risen unless he saw the marks of the nails in Jesus' hands and put his hand in the wound made by the soldier's spear as Jesus hung upon the cross (20:25). For this he has been labeled by tradition, "the doubting Thomas."

But Thomas was not so different. Most of us are just like him (or perhaps should be more like him). Many of us are not satisfied with believing on the basis of the reports of the experiences of other people. Young people especially are sometimes not satisfied to embrace a religious faith just because it is the faith of their parents. We modern Thomases hear the reports of the experiences of faith of others, but we ask why we should believe on the basis of secondhand reports. Like Thomas we will not believe until we see and touch that which convinces us.

That seems a reasonable request. We ought not be asked to base our whole lives on a religion which we know only second-hand. Otherwise we become (as someone has so vividly put it) like a man carrying a sandwich-board sign announcing a meal at a restaurant—a meal the man himself has never tasted and for which he hungers. We need experiences which point toward the truthfulness of a religion before we place our whole faith in it. We do not buy a car before we first drive it and test it out. If it runs well, if we kick the tires and they don't fall off, then we invest our money in the auto. Can we ask less of our religion? If we are to invest our lives in a religious faith, it is only reasonable that we test it and first find it worthy of our belief.

And Christianity is not a religion that demands faith without experience. The great leaders of the Christian church believed because of their experiences. Augustine felt himself invited to belief by an unusual event which caused him to explore the Scriptures. Martin Luther heard God's call in a terrible thunderstorm. John Wesley had his heart strangely warmed. And, in the beginning of this whole thing, something fearful and revealing happened to Paul as he made his way toward Damascus. Christianity is built on the experience of God's reality and his call to us. Thomas' demand is not only natural; it is eminently rational and justifiable.

But Thomas also demanded a physical, sensual experience of seeing and touching. And here again we identify with him. We naturally want a clear and unambiguous sign of the truthfulness of the faith, a sign of which we can be certain and which gives us confidence. We say, "If God is real and if he is love, let him show me in a way I can clearly understand." Amid the uncertainties of life, it is only natural that we seek such a certain experience. We want to believe the Easter message— that good triumphs in the end. Oh, how we would like to believe that, especially when evil seems to rape and slaughter the good in our world! But if that is true, let there be a concrete sign that that is indeed the case.

Young people today (and increasingly persons dissatisfied in mid-career) take vocational interest and aptitude examinations before they choose their vocations. An aspiring pastor in most of our major denominations today is required to take such examinations and demonstrate a propensity toward the skills of ministry before the church body will endorse that person for ordination. We want evidence—concrete, measurable evidence— before we believe that we will be good pastors, teachers, lawyers, business persons, or whatever. Again, Thomas' demand for an experience of the resurrected Christ is only natural, and we can identify and sympathize with it.

Thomas was fortunate: he received that experience for which he was asking. The risen Christ appeared to him, and Thomas believed. He had the experience that he was so much wanting.

Thomas then was one of those blessed with an experience that filled his needs and allowed him to believe.

THE POSITIVE ROLE OF DOUBT

The scandal of doubt seems not a scandal at all, but the natural and reasonable demand of a human. Or does it? Notice the role his doubt plays on his path to belief. It is his doubt which occasions his experience with Christ. He gives expression to his doubt. He "lets it all hang out." He does not believe the resurrected Christ has appeared to his colleagues. Only because of his doubt—and his willingness to face up to and express his doubts—does he find his demand met. Doubt is the threshold to belief for Thomas.

An interesting possibility. Doubt can play a positive role in the journey to faith. We would have thought otherwise. But John is insisting that doubt is not to be suppressed but expressed. Most of us want to play hide-and-seek with our doubts. We want to tuck them safely away out of sight and preferably out of mind. John is pointing us in a different direction. Through the Thomas narrative he is teaching a different strategy with regard to doubt. In a word, express your doubts, for they may lead you to new levels of faith.

Someone has said that doubts are like the measles: health is served if they come out. Doubt is comparable to anger. Anger is an unpleasant and negative feeling which most of us would like to avoid. So, when we do feel angry, we try to repress it, shove it deep within ourselves where it will not intrude into our milder and more pleasant emotions. But when we do that, the anger does not disappear; it resides deep within us and multiplies. Like yeast-filled dough, anger swells in size and degree. Repressed anger eventually explodes in rage. Captured within us and ignored, it increases until it bursts out of its psychical confinement and causes irrational and often regrettable behavior.

Doubt is much the same. A doubt left to ferment within us

only grows in size and degree. It feeds on itself, until it finally emerges from hiding to attack our faith. The trouble with captured and unacknowledged doubt is that it bursts forth in moments of crisis. When life presents us with one of those numerous challanges to faith, our repressed doubts attack us from the rear. Threatened outwardly by the crisis and flanked by our own doubts suddenly reemerged, we succumb and surrender.

Instead then of the spiritually neurotic practice of hiding our doubts, John invites us to be "doubting Thomases." Let your doubts be known. We can take a lesson, not only from John's portrayal of Thomas but also from several biblical characters who struggled with their doubts. Look at the prayers of Jeremiah. He did not hide his doubts from himself or from God, but expressed them openly and articulately. "You are to me," Jeremiah prays to God, "like a muddy swamp which cannot be trusted, like water that is poisoned" (15:18, my translation). Or, consider again the complaints of Job. Job never doubted God's existence, but he made quite clear how much he doubted the way in which God seemed to govern this world. And the book of Ecclesiastes is a compendium of the doubts of a wise and searching writer. The very fact that Ecclesiastes stands in the canon of our Scripture is evidence that our doubts have a vital role to play in the life of a believer.

Our analysis of doubt could go on. Paul Tillich argued with supreme persuasion that faith and doubt are not opposites but different sides of the same coin of belief. Without doubt, faith is not authentic, Tillich contended. Faith to be genuine must always stand in the presence of doubt—in the presence of the possibility that our faith may be wrong (See *The Dynamics of Faith*).

The scandal of doubt is that doubt of the truthfulness of this Easter reality we celebrate may be the positive catalyst which gives rise to authentic belief. Rather than destroying faith, it may be the birth pangs which accompany the new life of faith. We may doubt the reality of the resurrection of Christ. Easter may seem to us the most farfetched claim ever made by human thought. The scandal of doubt in this Easter narrative is that those reactions are admissible. They are okay. Don't hide them. Express them honestly and see what happens. We modern doubting Thomases may have the same experience as the original Thomas: we may have the truth of Easter brought immediately into the realm of our experience.

John has scandalized our preconceptions of doubt by structuring his climactic story of the resurrection appearance of Christ around the doubts of a disciple. He broadens our Easter perspective by insisting that doubt too can lead to the faith of Easter. But he intensifies the scandal of doubt by the *quality* of the faith which he shows can emerge from doubt. Christ appears to the disciples among whom this time is Thomas; and he invites Thomas to have that experience which in his doubt he had demanded (v. 27). In the presence of the resurrected Christ, Thomas' doubts crumble, and he cries out, "My Lord and my God!" (v. 28).

In his confession of faith, Thomas expresses what John would have us understand is the highest and most mature form of belief in Christ. In these words, Thomas is saying what John has been driving at for the previous 19 chapters: Jesus is no less than Lord and God. All the other confessions of belief in Christ pale in the presence of this supreme insight into the identity of Jesus. John identifies Christ with a variety of titles and descriptions throughout his gospel: Son of God and King of Israel (1:49), Christ and Messiah (4:25, 29), the Holy One of God (6:69), Son of Man (9:35-38), as well as others. But this confession of the "doubting Thomas" is the epitome of faith. By placing this confession in the concluding scene of his gospel, John is saying to us that all these other insights of faith lead to the confession that Jesus is Lord and God.

A word about these two titles is appropriate. That Jesus is called *Lord* may not seem unusual, for we find that expression again and again on the lips of persons addressing Jesus (see for example, 11:32; 13:6, 25). Actually the Greek term translated *Lord* is a term with two drastically different meanings, depend-

103

ing on the context. *Kyrios* was used in the sense of a polite form of address, such as "sir" (and so it is rendered in such places as 4:11; 5:7; and 12:20). But it was also the Greek word used to identify God—see Paul's use of it in Phil. 2:11. In the Greek translation of the Old Testament (called the Septuagint), *kyrios* is called upon to carry the meaning of the divine name of God in Hebrew—Yahweh. When *kyrios* appears on the lips of the disciples addressing Jesus in the gospel of John, the translators understandably render it, "Lord," instead of "sir." But in Thomas' confession it obviously carries its divine meaning, as is evident by the fact that it stands in association with the confession that Christ is God.

The expression of Thomas' faith that Jesus is God is beyond doubt the climax of this gospel we have been studying. It is rare, even in the New Testament, for Jesus to be called God. There is a reserve about this claim which seems to have made the early Christians hesitant to attribute this name even to Christ. The occurrences of the name of God for Christ are seldom found. (It occurs clearly only in Heb. 1:8-9; but even there it is within a psalm that is being quoted. Other passages in which it is less clear that the word *God* is attributed to Christ are Rom. 9:5; Col. 2:2; 2 Thess. 1:12; Titus 2:13; and 2 Peter 1:1. John contains the only unequivocal references.) But John has been leading his readers step by step toward this bold confession. He prepared us for this progress in the prologue of his gospel when he wrote, "and the Word was God" (1:1). (And perhaps, too, in 1:18 where the manuscript evidence is nearly as strong for the reading, "the only God," as it is for the reading, "the only Son.") And now he has that confession finally emerge on the lips of one of the disciples. With the affirmation of Thomas that Christ is God, John has bracketed his entire gospel with this claim—in the first sentence of his work and in the last scene.

John is telling us that the doubts of Thomas prepared the way for the recognition that Jesus was God! The climactic confession of the gospel is preceded with doubt. Easter is not a time for the repression of doubt, but the time to allow those doubts to lead us into a confrontation which will evoke from us the highest confession of all. The slogan, "It is always darkest just before the dawn," has doubtless been worn to shreds. Yet there is a truth in that statement which John seems indirectly to affirm. The darkness of Thomas' doubt is the foreshadowing of the dawn of his insightful faith. As difficult as this may be for us to see, it is this unusual and startling Easter message John announces to us.

THE BLESSEDNESS OF
FAITH WITHOUT SEEING

The scandal of doubt at Easter is offensive enough for us. But John pushes still further with a related aspect of that scandal. Notice the strange words with which Jesus responds to and affirms Thomas' confession: "Have you believed because you have seen me? Blessed are those who have not seen and yet believe" (v. 29).

Now, wait just a minute, Jesus! You've got that all wrong. The blessed ones are the ones who have had this kind of extraordinary experience of seeing Jesus. We make saints out of those who have had one of those rare experiences of miraculous vision. Their faith is rewarded and their blessedness affirmed by the fact that God chooses to reveal himself in some special way to them. It is those people who can point to an experience of unusual, extraordinary, and even miraculous qualities whom we call "blessed." We are conditioned to think the opposite of what Jesus says is true: the blessed ones in life are those who have had experiences of the marvelous works of God—healings, providential leadings, awesome experiences with nature, answered prayer, the sense of God's presence in worship. These are the people we think of as blessed.

Jesus' words are addressed not so much to Thomas as to those of us who are not so fortunate as to have had the experience Thomas had. It is addressed to those of us who have not been convinced of our religion because of wonders and miracles in our lives. It is addressed to those of us who think of ourselves not as the blessed ones but as the spiritual peons of Christianity. And his words startle us. *We* are the blessed ones! Those of us who go on believing without having seen—we are blessed. Jesus again reverses our conception of things.

John probably intended these words for the Christians of the second and third generations after Jesus, who thought that they had been shortchanged because their untimely life-spans had not allowed them to witness the historical Jesus or the resurrected Christ. John is saying to them that the blessed ones are not necessarily those fortunate enough to have witnessed the historical Jesus or to have had a vision of the resurrected Christ. Those who believe without those experiences are blessed.

This means that those of us who have not had the wondrous experiences are not at all second-class citizens of the kingdom of God. It means that those of us who have not had an Easter experience comparable to that of Thomas and the other disciples need not feel that we must sit in the back row of the kingdom. We are blessed if we believe without the experience of seeing.

This means, too, that religious experience is not the measure of the degree of God's blessings. In this day of the revival of emphasis upon Christian experience, the Johannine beatitude is vitally important. The evangelical Christians and the charismatic Christians are united in their testimony to marvelous experiences of God's presence. They make the rest of us wonder if our faith is authentic. But this word of Jesus suggests that we are the blessed ones afterall—those of us who have plodded along believing without benefit of all of those occurrences we hear other Christians talk about.

Maybe it is this kind of Christian life God most values: the life lived with doubt and yet with the struggling will to believe amid all of the uncertainties, the life lived without the annihilation of doubts by marvels and wonders. It would be easier to be one of those persons granted an extraordinary experience which makes believing inescapable. But it is harder, and hence more blessed, to be one of the "plodders" of Christianity. Believing without seeing is difficult, because it is so risky; there are none of those wondrous experiences upon which to rest your faith and from which to derive your assurance when the doubts seem too much to handle.

William Sloane Coffin has written about his own experience in coming to grips with his doubts and believing in spite of them. He tells of attending a funeral of a friend while in college. Shocked by his death, his doubts concerning Christianity seemed confirmed. But as he listened to the organist playing a Bach chorale, it occurred to him that religious truth, like great music, never eliminates the mystery of life but only deepens it. Faith never solves the mystery, it only leads one deeper into the darkness of mystery. Faith is not believing with or without evidence; it is trusting with our total being (*One to Every Man,* pp. 82-83). The blessedness of believing without seeing is just that we dare to trust and move into the midst of the mystery without confidence that we know where we will end up.

THE LIGHT IN THE DARKNESS

The scandal of doubt is complete now. Not only do we find Thomas' demand for a sign natural and reasonable; not only do we find that Thomas' doubt, when honestly expressed, led him to his experience of the resurrected Christ; we find, too, that we are the blessed ones if we can believe amid the morass of our doubts without having had the experience of Thomas. The Easter faith looks different from the perspective of John's story of this resurrection appearance. Now it looks like a faith that lives with doubt, yearns for and even demands the wondrous experience Thomas had, but stumbles on without seeing the resurrected Christ. Few of us this Easter will see the resurrected Christ. Many of us will not even leave this day with a cherished memory of a new and vital sense of Christ's living reality. We will go on beyond this Easter with our doubts still actively churning up their muddy waters of uncertainty.

But we will believe anyway. That is the scandal of doubt—
believing anyway.

A part of us doubts this Easter story. A part of us doubts
that good really triumphs over evil. A part of us doubts that
there is life beyond the shadows of death. A part of us may
even doubt that there is a God, much less the God who raised
Jesus from death. But we will believe *anyway.* And for that we
will be blessed!

There is a darkness generated by doubt. Strangely enough, our
little particles of faith do not lead us away from that darkness
but right into it. And amid that darkness we continue to grope
for the light switch that will illuminate the darkness and let
us see our way clearly. But it evades our grasp. The blessedness
of living a faith that has not seen and the blessedness of living
a faith in the darkness of doubt is precisely that continued
groping through the darkness. It is the willingness to take another step for another day, believing the resurrected Christ
stands beyond the threshold of the next dark doorway. It is
the blessedness of believing that the sparks of light in that
darkness are enough to venture a few more yards.

Years ago I was serving as chaplain for a small college in
the midwest. A handful of students had requested a weekly
service of Holy Communion. After searching frantically for
a time convenient for as many as possible, we finally settled
reluctantly upon 6:30 a.m. on Friday mornings. One dark, cold
winter Friday morning I arrived in the building at 6:00 a.m.
to prepare for the service. On this occasion, I had arrived ahead
of the janitor, and the building was engulfed in darkness. I
struggled my way down the halls in pitch blackness, wondering
where the light switches were and hoping I could make my
way to the chapel where I knew I could get the lights on. As
I felt my way around a turn, there was a light beaming through
the hallway. It was the light emitted by the ever-operative college
pop machine. Modest though it was, that light was enough for
me to find my way to the chapel and the light switches in that
room.

Preparing for the service, I could not escape the feeling that there was a parable in my experience. The darkness of this world is illumined only slightly and often from the most unusual and unexpected sources. And as I contemplated the celebration of the Eucharist, it occurred to me that the light of the world is emitted through the daily and mundane realities of our existence. The light is seldom the result of dramatic and marvelous experiences, but of the simple and ordinary things around us. The light of this darkened world is emitted through bread and wine. The resurrected Christ confronts us in such ordinary, daily things as pop machines, loaves of bread, and cups of wine.

"The light shines in the darkness, and the darkness has not overcome it" (1:15). Strange, isn't it, that John does not say the *light overcomes the darkness?* He affirms that the darkness is there and remains, even when the light shines persistently within the darkness. The darkness of our doubts remain. But the light of the resurrected Christ penetrates that darkness from time to time through the ordinary realities of our lives. That we find Christ in the sacrament of bread and wine suggests that we look for the light of the resurrected Christ precisely in the midst of our daily, mundane lives. This is the scandal of doubt—that we are to live with it and find amid the darkness of our doubts our risen Lord.

FOR FURTHER READING

Brown, Raymond E. *The Gospel According to St. John*. Garden City, N.Y.: Doubleday, 1966.

Bultmann, Rudolf. *The Gospel of John*. Philadelphia: Westminster, 1971.

Bultmann, Rudolf. *Jesus and the Word*. New York: Scribner, 1958.

Schnackenburg, Rudolf. *The Gospel According to St. John*. New York: Herder and Herder, 1968.

Tillich, Paul. *Dynamics of Faith*. New York: Harper, 1956.

Wesley, John. *Explanatory Notes upon the New Testament*. London: Epworth, 1958.